About the

Alexandra David-Neel was born in France. A student
of philosophy and oriental languages, she travelled widely in
Europe and then spent over twenty years in Tibet. Taught by
Buddhists and mystics she became an authority on Eastern
thought and the first European to stay in Lhasa, home of the
Dalai Lama. She died in Digne, France in 1969, aged 102.

Initiations and Initiates in Tibet

ALEXANDRA DAVID-NEEL

Authorised translation by
FRED ROTHWELL

RIDER
LONDON SYDNEY AUCKLAND JOHANNESBURG

Rider & Company Ltd

3 Fitzroy Square, London W1P 6JD

An imprint of the Hutchinson Publishing Group

London Melbourne Sydney Auckland
Wellington Johannesburg and agencies
throughout the world

First impression 1931
Second edition 1958
This edition 1970
Second impression April 1973

Typeset in Plantin Light by SX Composing DTP

Printed and bound in Great Britain by
The Guernsey Press Co. Ltd., Guernsey, Channel Islands

ISBN 0 09 032071 9

CONTENTS

Foreword   x

Introduction   xi

1 Tibetan Mysticism   1

2 The Various Kinds of Initiation and their Aim   28

3 Where Initiations Lead. The Different Meanings
   of *Aum Mani Padme Hum!*   71

4 Daily Spiritual Exercises   95

5 The Dalai Lamas   113

6 The Lesser and the Greater Vehicle   136

7 The True Initiation   152

8 The Different Types of Morality   161

9 The Cultivation of Attention   173

10 Cosmic Consciousness   183

11 The Teaching of Tibetan Mystics   190

12 The Tibetan Intelligentsia   224

   Appendix. A Note on the Present Position
   of the Dalai and Penchen Lamas   240

ILLUSTRATIONS

Alexandra David-Neel

The Lama Yongden

Alexandra David-Neel and her adopted son, the
  Lama Yongden

The present Dalai Lama

Lhassa: the Dalai Lama's palace

Alexandra David-Neel's hermitage in Tibet, about
  13,000 feet above sea level

A Tibetan anchorite who lives naked among the
  snowy mountains

A Tibetan initiate performing a *dubthab* rite in the
  forest

Statue of *Chenrezigs* in a Lamaist Temple

The altar of Lamaist temple

FOREWORD

The first edition of *Initiations Lamaïques* appeared twenty-six years ago, that is shortly after the publication of *Parmi les mystiques et les magiciens du Tibet*. The success of these two books – which were translated into several foreign languages – shows, I think, that the indifference professed by most of our contemporaries towards matters of a spiritual nature is far from being universal.

There are still many whose curiosity is great concerning the so-called esoteric doctrines taught by Masters who acknowledge traditions different from those which prevail in the West. Many of these "inquirers" are content with descriptions of strange rites or with the reading of formulae whose vague significance flatters a latent love of mystery. There are others, however, who display a more intelligent desire for information. They understand that all "esoterism" arises from misunderstanding and that rites, symbols and enigmatic pronouncements are merely a veil that is easy to raise for anyone who is fired with a keen desire to know.

The Tibetan spiritual Masters have never ignored this fact and their discipline has always tended to induce their disciples to come to grips with the real meaning of the teaching which is presented to them in language rich in ritual descriptions that partake of the nature of a rebus.

After the publication of *Initiations Lamaïques*, my adopted son, the late Lama Yongden, and I went back to Tibet and there stayed for twelve years. We were able in that country to study more deeply the conceptions of the Tibetan thinkers, conceptions relating to many subjects of practical utility for the guidance of our conduct in the arduous voyage of our lives. I have, therefore, thought it advisable to add two supplementary chapters to what was contained in previous editions of *Initiations Lamaïques* ("Initiations and Initiates in Tibet"). One of these chapters, founded on notes left by the Lama Yongden, deals with the essential importance of sustained attention and of memory in the spiritual discipline of Buddhism, the aim of which is the attainment of Knowledge.

In the other additional chapter I have set forth various theories that the Tibetan thinkers have elaborated concerning "Cosmic Consciousness" or, what is perhaps more rightly termed the "Universal Subconsciousness" present everywhere and in everything and that is efficient, even although its influence upon those who surround us and upon ourselves remains almost always unsuspected.

Finally, I have added a special chapter on the Tibetan Intelligentsia for the English edition.

Digne, B.A.,
France, 1958

Madame David-Neel died at her home in Digne in September 1969 at the age of 102.

INTRODUCTION

Since the profound changes which are taking place in Tibet seem likely to modify both the physical aspect and the spiritual atmosphere of the country so that, indeed, it may soon have lost its age-old appearance, that of a most strange land haunted by gods and by sages greater than gods, it may be interesting to present an account of the ideas that have originated in Tibet and of the practices to which these ideas have given rise.

Those few foreigners who have been in close contact with the mystical and philosophical thought of the Tibetans belong to a generation that is now fading away. It is desirable, therefore, to collect, with care, the information that such people have to offer; from this standpoint the following book may be regarded as a documentary volume.

The first English language edition of *Initiations and Initiates in Tibet* appeared in 1932 and followed translations of the French original presented in German and other foreign languages. During the twenty-six years that have elapsed since 1932, the writer, Alexandra David-Neel, and her adopted son, the Lama Yongden, made another prolonged stay in Tibet and in neighbouring regions, a sojourn that lasted no less than twelve years. This new edition of *Initiations and Initiates* presents a revised and considerably augmented text – the result of additional researches made by the author and her adopted son.

The reader's attention is drawn to a possible error which may be made if the word "Initiation" is taken to mean what it might if used in connection with the Mysteries of ancient Greece or Egypt.

In Tibet "initiation" is, first and foremost, a means calculated to induce the novice to discover *for himself* certain facts that are not directly revealed to him but which, by the aid of symbolical rites, he will eventually perceive himself. Tibetan initiation is not intended to enlighten the novice but rather to lead him to become conscious of what has hitherto been hidden from him because his mental eye has not been capable of perceiving it.

1

TIBETAN MYSTICISM

To present to Westerners a perfectly clear and complete idea of the mysticism of the Tibetans is almost impossible. There is a wide gulf between the various religious and philosophical conceptions which they accept and those which serve as basis for the meditations of the ascetics of the "Land of Snow". The very word mysticism, which I have used in a previous book and which I shall continue to use in this because I can find none better, must be understood, when dealing with Tibet, in a sense altogether different from the one we are accustomed to give it.

In the West, a mystic is a devout person – of a very superior type, granted, but always essentially a believer, the worshipper of a God. Such is, indeed, the definition given in the dictionaries. We can read in the French Larousse dictionary: "*Mysticism.* A philosophical and religious doctrine according to which perfection can be defined as a sort of contemplation which reaches ecstasy and mysteriously unites Man with the Deity."

On the contrary, the Tibetan mystic will probably be regarded by many Occidentals as an atheist. If we call him by such a name, however, we must guard against attributing to the term those feelings and ideas which it connotes in Western lands.

In countries under Christian influence the atheist, for centuries past, has been a rare exception, a kind of demoniacal character appearing in the flock of faithful believers. Even in these days he appears before the imagination of many as a rebel confronting Faith and Religion in a theatrical attitude of denial and challenge. There is nothing like this in Tibet where the idea of a supreme personal God has never held sway.

Among the numerous deities in the Lamaistic pantheon, there is not one that occupies the rôle of an eternal omnipotent Being, the creator of the world. These deities are regarded as belonging to one of the six species of conscious beings recognised by popular belief. The abodes assigned to them are not always situated outside of our earth. Besides, when their habitual sojourn is allocated to other regions of space, these latter, so the Tibetans believe, are sufficiently near the earth to enable the gods to intervene at every turn. And so prudence enjoins one to live on neighbourly terms with the less important of these gods, to enlist the favour of the more powerful and to receive clemency or neutrality from those of evil disposition, even to resist them.

This religion, compounded of an exchange of good services, testimonies of respect, and a lion-tamer's cunning, has nothing in common with the love that inflames certain Christian saints, still less with the passionate transports – so promptly degenerating into sensuality – of certain *bhaktas* of India.

Sprung from such an environment, dominating it though retaining the impression it has made upon his nature, the Tibetan contemplative is giving way to no sentimental impulse when he leaves the society of men and withdraws to the desert. Still less does he imagine that he is doing anything in the nature of a sacrifice.

In contradistinction to the Occidental who frequently enters the cloister after doing violence to his deepest affections, with tear-stained face painfully tearing himself away from what he still designates as the "good things" of this world, the Tibetan ascetic, like the Hindu *sannyâsin,* envisages renunciation as a happy deliverance.

Buddhist writings contain many passages descriptive of this state of mind:

"Home life is strict slavery, freedom consists in leaving home."

"In the eyes of the Tathâgata,[1] the splendour of a king is no more than spittle or a speck of dust."

"Full of charms are the lonely woods. Those who are freed delight in things that do not attract the populace."

No "rapture" awaits the sober thinker in his hermitage, his hut or cave, amid the immensity of Tibetan solitudes. Ecstasy, however, will be his for him to plunge himself therein. What will keep him in a state of attentive immobility day after day, month after month, and year after year, will be the contemplation of the working of his thought in self-analysis, effacing its own functionings according as they are discovered to be untrue, until the time comes when reasoning[2] ceases because it has been replaced by direct perception.

Then, the storms raised by thought-creating theories and speculations having calmed down, the ocean of the mind becomes tranquil and smooth, without a single ripple disturbing its surface. In this faultlessly smooth mirror things are

---

[1]Tathâgata – Tibetan Téjinshèkpa (dé bjin gshégs pa) "One who has gone on as his predecessors" (gone into Nirvâna). A title given to the Buddha Gautama, the historic Buddha.

[2]*Togpa,* more correctly "ratiocination", in opposition to *togspa* true understanding. (Tibetan spelling *rtogpa* and *rtogspa.*)

reflected without their image becoming distorted[1] – and this is the starting-point of a series of states which comprise neither ordinary consciousness nor unconsciousness. This is the entrance into a sphere different from that in which we habitually move; hence, after making a certain number of reservations as to the meaning of the term, we may speak of Tibetan "mysticism".

Whatever be the goal at which they aim, the most striking peculiarity of Tibetan mystics is their boldness and a singular impatient desire to measure their strength against spiritual obstacles or occult foes. They seem animated by the spirit of adventure and, if I may use the term, I should like to call them "spiritual sportsmen".

Indeed, this strange name suits them better than any other. Whatever branch of the mystic highway upon which they venture, the enterprise is an arduous and a perilous one. The sporting way in which they regard the fight is no ordinary religious attitude, and for that very reason it merits our attention.

Still, it would be erroneous to look upon as a hero each of those who desire acceptance of a *gyud lama*,[2] and demand his *Dam ngag*.[3]

Amongst the candidates for the preliminary initiations, specially original or otherwise remarkable individuals form a small minority; most of them are simple monks. Large numbers of them, before seeking more esoteric teaching, have not even attempted to acquire the instruction given in the

---

[1] The ocean and the mirror are frequently compared together by Tibetans, Hindus, and Chinese.

[2] *Gyud lama* does not here mean a graduate of the school of *gyud* (ritual magic), but rather a master supposed to be the guardian of secret institution.

[3] *Dam ngag*: "precepts and ounsels".

monastic schools.

The cause of this neglect may be a lack of faith *a priori* in the value of this official science; nevertheless, it is quite possible that the regular study of the books may simply have been deemed too arduous for a considerable number of those who turn away.

Instinctive tendencies to contemplation and the sheep-like imitation of the examples set by others are the origin of the vocation of many a *naldjorpa*.[1]

A man thinks only of "making religion",[2] as it is called in Tibetan, without his having the faintest idea where the path upon which he has entered may lead him.

All the same, he who was a mere simpleton at the outset of his mystical career is not condemned to remain one always. Unexpected miracles are frequent on the "Short Path."[3] Here the blind man becomes clairvoyant and the clairvoyant loses his eyesight. Disciples of torpid intellect sometimes become transformed into far-seeing investigators, whereas brilliant intellects sink into a condition of dull stupor.

The tremendous speed with which the mental, moral and even physical worth of an individual changes is amazing to behold. And yet the Tibetan mystics remain unperturbed. The germs to which these apparently incoherent transformations are due, they assert, exist in the various individuals. Hitherto

[1] *Naldjorpa* (written *rnal byorpa*) means literally: "He who is possessed of perfect serenity." In ordinary language, this means an adept in the doctrines of the "Short Path," often also an ascetic supposed to possess super-normal psychic powers.

[2] *Chös Ched* (written *chos byed*).

[3] On the subject of the "Short Path", see *With Mystics and Magicians in Tibet*, p. 243. There we find the doctrine and the resultant methods whereby, according to the Tibetans, it is possible to reach Buddhahood in the very life that a man begins his spiritual training, without having to progress slowly after the ordinary mode of successive rebirths.

there had simply been lacking the conditions favourable to their growth and fructification.

The aspirant after mystical initiation must, from the very outset, cultivate discernment and the power to assume the attitude of a calm and detached observer,[1] capable of complete mastery over natural inclinations and fleeting appetites. No ordinary skill is required to follow successfully the perilous training imposed on some disciples – a training which consists in the full experience of various passions. Here it is a question of entering fire and not being singed. The tests to which certain disciples submit on the advice of their spiritual guide or impelled by the desire to prove their mental strength are extremely original and the result of them is scarcely credible, especially as regards the mastery of carnal instincts.

The disciple is also recommended to observe the acts he performs, the awakening within himself of thoughts and sensations, attractions, and repulsions, to endeavour to discover their causes, then the causes of these causes, and so on.[2]

In the opposite direction, consideration must be given to the chain of effects susceptible of following the various material or mental acts.

From all this it is easy to see that, under the names of esoteric or mystical methods, Lamaists really include a positive psychic training. Indeed, they look upon salvation not as the gift of a deity, but rather as an arduous conquest and the means of attaining salvation they regard as a science.

Consequently, just as we go to a professor when we wish

---

[1] The following passage from the *Mundakupanishad* may serve to illustrate this attitude: "Two inseparable birds perch upon the branch of a tree. One of them eats the fruit of the tree; the other, without touching the fruit, watches his companion." This parable was intended to explain the Vedantic doctrine of *jîva*, but it is equally appropriate here.

[2] See Chapter 9 on Attention.

to learn mathematics or grammar, Tibetans naturally have recourse to a master of mysticism when they desire to be initiated into spiritual methods.

The Sanskrit word *guru* is the name given to the spiritual guide, and the Tibetans have admitted this foreign word into their literary vocabulary. In conversation, however, they generally say "My Lama", the possessive adjective being understood as indicating the relation between a master and a disciple.

Although the Tibetans pay for the knowledge communicated to them by the utmost respect and material assistance, it is rare to find in their country that blind worship of the *guru* which is so common in India.

Milarespa, the anchorite poet, was an exception. Examples of such fervour as he manifested, his admiration for and devotion to his master, are rare.

In spite of many hyperbolical expressions used in their speech to or concerning him, the veneration of a Tibetan disciple is really given to the knowledge of which the master is the guardian. With few exceptions, the disciples are fully aware of the shortcomings of "their Lama", but respect keeps them from confiding to another their discoveries in this direction. Besides, many things which would appear reprehensible to a Westerner do not shock them in the least.

Not that the Tibetans, speaking generally, are destitute of moral principles, but the latter are not necessarily the same as those practised in our own countries. Polyandry, for instance, which is often so sternly judged in the West, does not appear to them culpable in the slightest; on the other hand, marriage between relatives – even between cousins far removed – seems to them abominable whereas we see in it no harm whatsoever.

When Tibetans sometimes pay lavish homage to a man whose imperfections are evident, in many cases this attitude is not caused by blindness to his defects.

To understand it we must remember how different are Western ideas concerning the "ego" from those held by the Buddhists.

Even when they have rejected belief in an immaterial and immortal soul regarded as their true "ego", most Occidentals continue to picture to themselves a homogeneous entity which endures from birth to death at least. This entity may undergo change, may become better or worse, but it is not supposed that these changes must follow one another from minute to minute. Thus, failing to observe the manifestations which break the continuity of a person's habitual aspect, we talk of a man who is good or bad, austere or dissolute, etc. . . .

The Lamaist mystics deny the existence of this "ego". They assert that it is no more than a concatenation of transformations, an aggregate whose elements, material and mental alike, act and react upon one another and are incessantly being exchanged for those of the neighbouring aggregates. Thus the individual, as they see him, is like the swift current of a river or the many aspects of a whirlpool.

Advanced disciples are able to recognise, amid this succession of individuals showing themselves in their master, the one from whom useful lessons and counsels may be obtained. In order to profit thereby, they tolerate the inferior manifestations which appear to them in the same Lama, just as they would patiently await the passing of a sage in a crowd of people.

One day I related to a Lama the story of the Reverend Ekai Kawaguchi[1] who, desirous of learning the Tibetan grammar, had applied to a famous master. The latter belonged to

[1]The Venerable Ekai Kawaguchi was a learned Japanese Buddhist and told this adventure in the account of his stay in Tibet.

the religious Order and gave himself out to be a *gelong*.[2] After staying with him a few days, the pupil discovered that his professor had transgressed against the law of celibacy and was the father of a little boy. This fact filled him with such profound abhorrence that he packed up his books and belongings and took his departure.

"What a booby!" exclaimed the Lama on hearing the anecdote. 'Was the grammarian less skilled in grammar for having given way to the temptations of the flesh? What relation is there between these things and in what way did the moral purity of his professor concern the student? The intelligent man gleans knowledge wherever it is to be found. Is not that man a fool who refuses to pick up a jewel lying in a dirty vessel because of the filth adhering to the vessel?"

Enlightened Lamaists regard the veneration shown to their spiritual guide from the psychic point of view.Indeed, they regard worship of every kind from the same standpoint.

While acknowledging that the instruction of an expert in spiritual matters is extremely valuable and useful, many of them are inclined to make the disciple himself largely responsible for the success or failure of his spiritual training.

Here we are not concerned with the zeal, the power of concentration or the intelligence of the neophyte. The usefulness of these is self-evident. Another element, however, is deemed necessary, and even more potent than all the others. This element is faith.

Not only the mystics of Tibet but numerous Asiatics believe that faith is a power in itself. It works independently of the intrinsic value of its object. The god may be a stone, the spiritual father an ordinary man, and yet the worship of them

[2]*Gelong*, written *dge slong*, literally a virtuous medicant, the approximate Lamaistic equivalent of the *bhikkhu* of the Southern Buddhists: a celibate monk who has received the major ordination.

may awaken in the devotee unsuspected energy and latent faculties.

External testimonies of respect, in the worship of the *guru* as in all other worship, aim at nourishing and intensifying faith and veneration.

Many novices who would never have dared to venture along the mystic path, had they not believed that they were sustained and upheld by the mental or magical power of their Lamas, have, in reality, been relying only upon themselves all the time. Nevertheless, the confidence they reposed in their master has produced an effect similar to that which might have been derived from external assistance.

There are stranger cases. Some occasionally give themselves up to devotional practices or other similar functions, though quite convinced that the object of their worship is non-existent. Nor is this insanity, as one might be tempted to believe, but rather the proof of a profound knowledge of psychic influences and of the power of auto-suggestion.

Certain Catholics extol a method which, at first sight, appears analogous. This consists in inducing an unbeliever to practise all the rites of their religion, in order to bring him within the fold.

One may imagine that the "unbelief" of the man who lends himself to this practice, with the object of eventually coming to believe, is not very serious and that he is lacking in deep conviction; hence the success of a stratagem which he himself wishes to succeed.

Among the Lamaists it is totally different. They do not try to believe. The gymnastics they practise tend simply to produce in them certain states of consciousness which the believers imagine to be due to the goodwill of their God or their *guru*, whereas they are a result of the practice itself, the physical act influencing the mind.

The mystic Masters of Tibet have minutely studied the effects upon the mind of bodily attitudes and gestures, of facial expression, also the influence of surrounding objects. A knowledge of these methods is part of their secret science. They utilise it in the spiritual training of their disciples. This science was known to the great Catholic "*gurus*". It may be found in the spiritual exercises of Saint Ignatius Loyola.

CHOICE OF A MASTER

Those who desire to place themselves under the direction of a spiritual guide are strongly recommended by the learned doctors of Lamaism to appeal to their utmost power of discernment in choosing the master best suited to them.

To the mind of a Tibetan, erudition, sanctity, and profound mystical conceptions are no guarantee that a Lama's counsels will be alike profitable to all his disciples. Each one, according to his character, must be directed along a different path by a master who has either traversed it himself or at all events studied it with sufficient minuteness to have acquired complete knowledge of the ground.

The candidate for initiation is generally ready to follow this prudent advice. Great is the difference between him and the ordinary monk lacking initiative, of whom there are thousands. Whereas the latter, from the day when, as a child, he was taken to the monastery, has simply advanced unthinkingly in the direction traced for him by his guardian, listlessly attending the classes of a monastic college or vegetating in a sort of sanctimonious ignorance, the future initiate shows that he possesses determination of his own. He has made up his mind to renounce the easygoing existence of the regular members of a *gompa*,[1] in order to risk the dual adventure of

[1] *Gompa*, written *dgompa*, "a dwelling in the solitude", is a name given to Tibetan monasteries.

surmounting difficulties of a spiritual nature and of confronting the material problem of his livelihood, in regions perhaps too far removed from his native land for him to benefit by the assistance which relatives and friends eagerly give to those who don the religious garb.

The young monk has almost invariably passed his twentieth year when he experiences his first faint desires to leave the monastery. Unlike the mystics of the West who retire to a cloister when the call from on high makes itself heard by them, the first effect of mystical tendencies in Orientals is to incline them to forsake the cenobitic life and seek isolation in a hermitage.

Endowed at this age with sufficient strength of character to make so important a resolution, the aspirant is certainly able to obtain information, and, according to the particular object he is pursuing, to appeal to a Lama whose known disciples have been spurred along in a similar direction.

All the same, there are cases when such an investigation cannot take place: the first meeting of some with the *guru* whose disciples they are to become seems a pure matter of chance.

Not only has the future disciple never heard speak of this Lama, he has never even conceived the idea of devoting his life to the pursuit of a religious object. Nevertheless, within the space of an hour, or even more suddenly, everything is changed and he embarks for the mysterious world through which "the stream makes for itself a channel".[1]

Of course, the word "chance" which I have just used is not to be found in the vocabulary of convinced determinists like the Lamaists. These unforeseen meetings and their conse-

---

[1] "To enter the stream" is a frequently used expression of Buddhistic terminology. It means to take the first step in the spiritual life which will lead to illumination, to Buddhahood.

quences they regard as due to distant causes in previous lives.

It often happens that a master advises a candidate or even an already accepted disciple to go to another Lama. This advice is given because the master looks upon his method as unsuited to the particular character of the student. At other times, however, the *guru* declares that, as the result of a sort of clairvoyance manifesting itself during his meditations, he has discovered that there are no spiritual bonds or psychic affinities between himself and his disciple, whereas the latter is psychically related to the Lama to whom he is sending him.

These bonds and affinities, whose origin the Lamaists trace to associations formed during past lives, are deemed practically indispensable to the disciple's success.

It is explained to certain other candidates that they are not yet ready to enter the mystic path, and the Lama benevolently counsels them to adopt some other course. Lastly, others are refused admission without any reasons being assigned as to the motives which have influenced the master.

Long preliminaries always accompany the reception of a candidate as an accepted disciple. These comprise a number of tests of a more or less severe character. Certain *gurus*, chiefly anchorites, convert this time into a sort of tragedy.

Instances of this I have given in a previous book; and accordingly I regard it as useless to weary the reader with repetitions here.

We must now examine what the young religious élite of Tibet so fervently solicit from the masters of mysticism.

Enlightened Lamas unanimously assert that the doctrines of all the schools of philosophy in their land – indeed, the entire Buddhic teaching – are set forth in books and publicly taught by professors in the monastic colleges of philosophy.[1]

---

[1]The *Tsen ñid* college – one of the four divisions of the Lamaistic universities.

The study of these different theories, their attentive examination, the reflections and meditations to which they give rise, may lead to an acquisition of the "Knowledge" by the one who devotes himself to them. And yet, according to the Tibetans, it is to be feared that this knowledge will remain a mere intellectual acceptance of the words alone or of the results of others' experiences. Now this kind of knowledge is regarded by them as very far removed from perfect understanding and realisation, the fruits of a direct personal apprehension of the object of knowledge.

It is interesting to note that the Tibetans have translated the title of the famous work attributed to Nâgârjuna: the *Prajñâ pâramitâ*, not as "Excellent knowledge", but as "Going beyond knowledge". Whether they are right or have taken too great liberties with the grammar, the fact remains that upon this "going beyond", they have built up an entire philosophical and mystical system – one in perfect agreement, after all, with the doctrines of the Buddhic school of the Mâdhyamka which holds sway in Tibet.

Great importance is attached to this "going beyond" in esoteric teachings. They comment in many ways on the "going beyond" charity, patience, vigilance, morality, serenity, knowledge. It must be understood that "beyond" the narrow and unenlightened conceptions we have of charity, etc., there exists another way of understanding and practising them. At a higher stage of initiation, the insignificance of this second way of understanding charity, etc., is in its turn exposed.

Then we come to the enigmatical declarations of *The Diamond Cutter*:[1] "It is when one no longer believes in anything whatsoever that the time has come to make gifts."

---

[1] *Dordje chödpa* (*rdorjé gchod pa*) a very popular work in Tibet. It is the translation of the Sanskrit *Vajracchedika*.

We may suppose that the mental trend of the Tibetans, perhaps, too, some traditions prior to the preaching, in their land, of the doctrines of the Uma school[1] inclined them towards this interpretation of the "excellent virtues" (the *pâramitâs*). Does the very text of the Prajñâpâramitâ give support to their system of "beyond"? That is a question too technical to be considered here.

It is generally admitted by Lamaists that knowledge (*shesrab*), if it is to be effective, must be combined with method, with skilful means (*thabs*) of bringing about the desired illumination.

The combined *thabs-shesrab* plays a predominant part in Lamaism. It is symbolically represented by a *dordji* (thunderbolt) and a tiny bell (*tilpu*).[2] The *dordji* is male and represents method, the hand-bell is female and represents knowledge.

The *naldjorpas* initiates wear rings adorned with these two emblems: a *dordji* on the gold ring worn on the right hand; a tiny bell on the silver ring worn on the left hand.

In mysticism, *thabs* and *shesrab* become *yab* and *yum*, i.e. father (method) and mother (knowledge). Thus must be interpreted the statues representing entwined couples which are to be seen in Lamaist temples.

In this connection, it is curious to note that certain foreigners betake themselves to the great temple of the Lamas at Pekin to sate their propensities for puerile obscenity by feasting their eyes upon these statues.

The sacristans of the place – whose mental attitude is that of all sacristans of temples visited by worldly minded tourists – have not failed to note the curiosity of visitors and to profit

---

[1]Written *dbuma* (of the middle). Translation of the Sanskrit *mâdhyamika*.
[2]Written *drilbu*.

thereby. With this object in view, in the temples to which visitors are admitted they have veiled the statues that interest them more particularly. Of course a gratuity is required for raising the curtain, and whilst the simple-minded traveller is staring with all his eyes, the cunning cicerone pockets a coin and smiles behind his back. I discovered this fact whilst living at Pei-lingsse, a Chinese monastery adjoining that of the Lamas. It is unnecessary to say that in Tibet veils are unknown. The symbol of the *yab* and the *yum* crowned with skulls and dancing upon corpses is there regarded as terribly austere.

These couples also represent void and desire, and various other philosophical ideas.

Method and knowledge and their indispensable union are also recalled by the ritual gestures designated *cha gya*[1] performed during the religious ceremonies with thunderbolt and tiny bell.

Though there is no esotericism whatsoever as regards philosophical knowledge, the same cannot be said regarding method. What is so fervently sought from masters of mysticism and sometimes acquired at the cost of incredible trials, is their *dam ngag* or *men ngag*,[2] i.e. advice and spiritual direction; also the *kha gyud* or *tam gyud*[3]: the traditional mystical teaching which is transmitted orally and must never be set down in writing.

Counsel and instruction are divided into several categories, such as: *gom*[4] *gyi men ngag* counsel on meditation dealing with the methods calculated to enable one to reach the goals set forth in the philosophical doctrines; *men-ngag zambo*

---

[1]Written *phyag rgya*. In Sanskrit *mûdra*.
[2]Respectively written *dgams ngag* and *man ngag*. Equivalent to the Sanskrit word *upadesha*.
[3]Written *bkah rgyud* and *gtam rgyud*.
[4]Written *bsgom*.

"profound advice" of the most lofty and secret nature, related to the final mysteries of the "Short Path" and to the manner of attaining Buddhahood. There is also "advice" relating to ritual, to medical science, to the art of preparing medicine, etc.

One special section of secret instruction deals with magic, whilst certain Lamas specialise in training their disciples in the various forms of breathing practices, technically designated *rlung*[1] *gom* of which there are many.

The term *dam ngag* is the most usual of those quoted, practically including them all. It is interpreted – as has already been stated – as instruction handed down from Master to disciple along a spiritual lineage.

Most initiates do not teach what they have learned; they even keep secret the fact that they have been initiated. They have taken an oath of silence regarding both these points, and this oath contains such dreadful imprecations that the perjurer would be reborn in the *nyalwas*.[2]

Those alone who have received an express injunction from their master can lawfully teach in their turn. Several disciples of a Lama may be permitted or commanded to communicate his *dam ngag* to carefully tested candidates. Nevertheless, as a general rule, the continuation of the *lob*

---

[1] The *r* is mute. I have retained it in order to avoid confusion between this word, meaning wind or breath, and the word *Lung*, which means "advice," and is also the term applied to many lower initiations.

[2] Written *dmyalba*: the worlds of affliction, generally called "hells" by Western writers. Popular Buddhism distinguishes between several of these. Still, seeing that their inhabitants are subject to death, after which they may be reborn under better – or altogether good – conditions, the term "purgatory" would seem to be more correct. The dwellers in the *nyalwas* are not necessarily animated by evil feelings. They are capable of compassionate thoughts and lofty feelings. It is said that the result of these latter is generally immediate death which frees these unhappy beings from their torment and secures them a happy rebirth. The initiates look upon these descriptions as symbolical and relating to realities of a spiritual nature.

gyud,[1] i.e. of the line of gurus, is entrusted to the most eminent of the spiritual sons of each of them. To him alone are taught, in their entirety, the doctrines and methods which his Lama received under the same conditions.

This way of transmitting traditional doctrines is not peculiar to Lamaism. It would appear to have existed in India even before the time of the Buddha. The Bönpos of Tibet boast that they possess a secret instruction that has been handed down orally for thousands of years.

The most famous line of masters is the one which, tradition relates, began with Mahâkashyapa, a direct disciple of the Buddha, and continued to Bodhidharma, i.e. for a period of slightly over one thousand years.[2] The lists of the successive masters of this spiritual dynasty, named "patriarchs," contain sometimes twenty-seven and sometimes twenty-eight names.

There is nothing unlikely in the supposition that Mahâkashyapa, and after him a number of Ancients, exercised considerable moral authority amongst the Buddhists. All the same, this was not altogether a transmission of doctrine, for the list of the "patriarchs" contains men who professed different opinions and whose disciples engaged in passionate controversy against one another.

A more authentic line of mystical masters began in China with Bodhidharma, founder of the Ts'an (meditation) sect which, being subsequently imported into Japan, was there called *Zen-shu*.

It was, say the Zen scholars of Japan, to establish on a firm footing the authority of Bodhidharma and his successors that a legend regarding the origin of the lineage of the "patriarchs" was invented by some ultra-zealous devotee – probably

[1]Written *slob rgyud*.
[2]The date of Buddha's death is given by the Buddhists of Ceylon as 544 BC, Bodhidharma arrived in China about AD 520.

a Chinese – about the ninth or tenth century of our era.

This legend does not refer merely to the tradition of some particular teaching but also to the way of promulgating it; for this reason more especially is it interesting to us.

The Buddha, it is said, happened once to be seated, with a large number of disciples about him, on the Vultures' Peak, near the town of Rajagriha.[1] A god came to bow before him, offering him a celestial golden flower. The Buddha took the flower and looked at it in silence.

None present understood what he meant except Mahâkashyapa, who smiled at him. The Buddha then declared: "I held the thought of Nirvâna which is the eye of the doctrine; this I now transmit to Mahâkashyapa."

The unwonted manner in which instruction is given and received in this legend sanctions the similar method used by the adepts of the "meditation" sect founded by Bodhidharma.

Bodhidharma was an Indian Buddhist belonging to the Brahmin caste. His methods of teaching differed widely from those of other masters. Esteeming erudition but slightly, he extolled introspective meditation as the true means of attaining to spiritual enlightenment. Shortly after his arrival in China, he withdrew to the monastery of Shao-ling.[2] There he spent most of his time in meditation, facing a wall of rocks. Some of his Chinese and Korean disciples, and those in Japan of the subdivision of the *Zen-shu* named *Soto*, have retained the habit of facing a wall during meditation.

The most eminent disciple of Bodhidharma was a Confucian scholar named Chang Kwang. He is said to have

[1]A town situated in the region now called Bihar.
[2]Situated in the mountains of the province of Honan. This historic spot appears to have been quite neglected by the disciples of Bodhidharma, numerous though they are in China and Japan. When I visited it, the monastery was partially in ruins.

gone to the abode of Bodhidharma to ask him to be his guide, and as the master for several days refused to receive him, he cut off his left arm and sent it to Bodhidharma in testimony of the zeal with which he was consumed.

Six patriarchs succeeded Bodhidharma in China as chiefs of the Ts'an sect, then the line split into two branches which also subsequently became subdivided.

The special methods and doctrines of the meditation sect were introduced into Japan in the sixth century and afterwards firmly established by En-sai in the eleventh century. The *Zen-shu* is still flourishing and counts many adherents among the intellectual élite of Japan. It is to be regretted, however, that here as well as in China the meditation sect has fallen back into the ritualism so sternly condemned both by Bodhidharma and by the Buddha himself.

In Tibet we find this instruction by telepathy. The mystics of the land distinguish between three classes of masters which are expressly designated in the liturgical formulas of certain rites. These are *Gongs gyud, Da gyud,* and *Nien gyud.*[1]

Gongs gyud is the "line of thought", whose masters teach by telepathy, without the aid of speech.

Da gyud is the "line of gestures", whose masters teach in silence, by gestures and signs.

Nien gyud is the line wherein the masters are "heard," i.e. they give their lessons in the ordinary way, speaking to their disciples who listen to them.

The telepathic method is regarded as the highest, but many Lamas believe that there are no longer, in these modern times, masters capable of practising it, nor even disciples sufficiently developed psychically to be capable of receiving instructions in this way. They think the same regarding

[1]Written: *dgongs brgyud – brdah brguyd – ñan brguyd.*

instruction by gestures, which comes second in their esteem.

Possibly the mystics who practised telepathic instruction were more numerous in past centuries than they are now. It is difficult to learn anything definite on this point. However it be, instruction by telepathy has certainly not wholly disappeared from Tibet. It is still practised by certain contemplatives, and so a considerable part of this method is also to be found in the rites that accompany the initiations into the higher degrees.

Amongst the guardians of mystic traditions it is fitting to mention the line of the *Kahgyudpas*, the sect of the "lineal transmission of orders or precepts".

Its spiritual ancestors are two Hindus, Tilopa of Bengal and Narota of Kashmir, both of whom lived about the tenth century.

It is uncertain who taught Tilopa the *dam ngag* which was subsequently imported into Tibet by a disciple of Narota, the Lama Marpa. Instead of a probable narrative we have nothing but a legend which is largely symbolical.[1]

In addition to his fantastic initiation by a Dâkini, the Tibetans believe that he was instructed by the mythical Dordje Chang, or even that he was an emanation of this latter. The same thing is said of the Lama Marpa who, as we have just stated, introduced the teachings of Narota into Tibet.

In his turn, Marpa communicated this *dam ngag* to the famous ascetic, the poet Milarespa (eleventh century) who imparted it to his disciple Tagpo Lhadje.[2]

Later on the line divided into six sects and sub-sects, the two most important of which are the *Karma Kahgyud* and the *Dugpa Kahgyud*. The former, whose name is generally abridged to that of *Karmapas*, constitute one of the most

---

[1]This strange legend is to be found in *With Mystics and Magicians in Tibet*, p. 167.
[2]Dwagpo Lhardje – the doctor Dwagpo.

important sects of the "Red Caps". Their chief abode, the residence of one of the spiritual descendants of Tilopa, is at Tolung Tsurpug, in the mountains, to the west of Lhasa.

As regards the *Dugpa Kahgyuds*, some authors have utterly mistaken their character by looking upon the term *dugpa* as indicating a sorcerer who practises a terrible form of black magic.

Dug (written *hbrug*) signifies thunder. The Dugpa sect, comprising those of the Centre and the South, dates from the twelfth century. It was founded by a disciple of Tagpo Lhadje, the Lama Chödje Tsangpa Gyarespa, sometimes called Tulku Pasgam Wangpo.

Tradition states that when this latter began to build the monastery of Ralung, a violent storm suddenly arose. Looking upon this incident as an omen, the Lama gave the name of "Thunder" to the new monastery. The monks who took up their quarters there, and subsequently all belonging to the same sect, were called "Those of the Thunder" (*dugpas*).

The monks of the Dug-Ralung became famous for their learning. They preached their doctrine in Bhutan (Himâlaya) and there set up monasteries. This caused the district to be called *Dug yul* (the Land of Thunder), the name still given to it by its inhabitants and the Tibetans.

Thus we see that *Dugpa* applies alike to the natives of Bhutan and to the followers of one of the sub-sects of the *Kahgyudpas*. This is not a sect of "Black Magicians" whose doctrine is "dugpism", as I have heard it called by certain foreigners. Indeed, the three principal Lamaist sects now existing: the *Gelugspas* ("yellow caps"), the *Kahgyudpas* (including the *Dugpas*), and the *Sakyapas* (the two latter being "red caps") – all have one common spiritual ancestor in the Hindu philosopher Atisha.

The spiritual lineage, continuing from Master to disciple, has almost everywhere in Tibet been supplanted by the line of *tulkus*,[1] and in some cases by hereditary succession.

For long the chief of the *Sakyapas* has been a married Lama whose son will succeed him. The head of the monastery of Mindoling, the grand Lama of the Dzogchénpas,[2] is a bachelor monk. On his death, he is succeeded by the eldest son of his lay brother. Should this latter die childless, the Lama would have to marry his widow in order to continue the dynasty.

These two cases, however, are exceptional. The enthusiasm of the Tibetans for the *tulkus* system is so great that there are now very few sects whose chief is not regarded as being always the same Lama who reincarnates and resumes his position after each of his deaths.

It is unnecessary to say that the change in the mode of continuing the lineage of religious Masters has proved prejudicial to the intellectual and moral status of the worshippers. Chiefs of sects and monasteries, who have been acknowledged as such when children do not always, on becoming adult, prove themselves to be endowed with the qualities requisite in a spiritual guide. Quite frequently they feel no inclination for this rôle and prefer the far easier one of a quasi-divine person whose sole task consists in receiving the homage of the devout . . . and their gifts.

Apart from these usurpers of titles to which they have no

---

[1] See *With Mystics and Magicians in Tibet*[2] p. 113.

[2] The latest of the Lamaistic sects founded in the seventeenth century. Mindoling (written *smin grol gling*) that is "the place where liberation matures" is in southern Tibet not far from the southern bank of the Yesru Tsangpo (the Brahmaputra). Another monastery of the same sect (whose Grand Lama is considered as their religious leader by all the *Dzogchénpas* of eastern and northern Tibet) lies on the border of the great grassy desert and the province of Kham. In my *With Mystris and Magicians in Tibet* I give a description of my visit to this monastery which I stayed at after I left Lhasa.

right, there are in Tibet some Lamas who are the authentic successors of a more or less ancient line of venerable Masters and who claim to be possessed of certain secret traditional teachings. These include men of lofty character whose methods seem to be the genuine result of prolonged periods of psychic experiences. Most of them live as hermits and remain faithful to the old system of succession from master to disciple.

Tibetan mystics occasionally – though very seldom – have recourse to another method of continuing a line of Masters: that of procreating a child with the object of making him an initiate and the successor of his father or of his father's *guru*.

The birth of such a child requires that a number of conditions be satisfied. In the first place, the future parents must have received from their Lama, the actual head of the line, the express order to engender a son who will carry out this task. This applies to the case in which the Lama's most eminent disciple, or one of those coming immediately after him, is married – a thing which may happen amongst the "Red Caps", where celibacy is not strictly enjoined in all the members of the clergy. A lay disciple of the Lama might also be chosen, but though this may be permitted in theory, instances of the fact are scarcely ever found except in legends.

When the master, obeying reasons with which he alone is acquainted, orders one of his bachelor disciples to become a father, the latter must seek a wife in accordance with the Lama's instructions. The woman chosen is generally one of those regarded as incarnate fairies: she must be marked with certain signs which may escape the notice of the ordinary person though evident enough to initiates. As the sole object of this union is the birth of a son destined to continue the *lob gyud* – the line of Masters – both husband and wife generally separate and live as monk and nun, once the child is born.

A special *angkur*[1] is conferred on the couple by "their Lama" in consecration of their union and generally, if the couple are not already married, they dispense with the usual marriage ceremony. Then both remain separately in the retreat for a longer or shorter period: several months, perhaps a whole year. During this time of reclusion they perform various rites, evoke the Changchub Semspas[2] and the holy Lamas, the ancestors of the line to which the husband belongs, and implore their blessing. By meditation they endeavour to establish a psychic bond between them and the most holy and enlightened elements in the whole world.

By this process, both the physical and the spiritual essence of the future parents is said to be refined and transformed. When their retreat is at an end, a new *angkur* is conferred upon them and their union takes place as a sacrament in the midst of a *kyilkhor* (magic circle).

Whatever may be thought of its efficacy, no one can deny the purely idealistic character of such eugenics.

Other methods have been imagined aiming at the same end, though involving coarse – and from our point of view utterly repulsive – practices, which symbolise the relation of father to son established between the parents' master and the child that is to be born.

Tradition says that this realistic rite was performed by Marpa for his married disciple, Ngog Chösdor. Because of its singular aspects, I will take the liberty of describing it briefly.

When their retreat had come to an end, the initiations having been duly conferred on both husband and wife, the *kyilkhor* erected and all the ceremonies concluded, Marpa shut

---

[1]Written *dbang skur*; literally "communication of power".
[2]Written *byang tchub sems pa*; in Sanskrit, bodhisattva.

himself up with his own wife Dagmedma and the young couple in his private oratory. There the Lama took his place on his
ritual throne along with his fairy-wife, whilst Ngog Chösdor
and his wife remained folded in each other's arms at his feet.
Marpa received his sperm in a goblet made of a human skull
and after mixing with it various ingredients supposed to possess magical properties, the potion was drunk by the disciple
and his wife.

This practice is based on the belief common to many
primitive nations that some particular occult virtue dwells in
animal seed. Actually it is his very energy and life that the *guru*
intends to transmit to the child about to be conceived for the
purpose of being his successor.

This strange rite is known only to very few Lamas. From
the information I have been able to gather, it is very seldom
performed. Only those, it is said, who have been initiated into
the profoundest secrets of a certain category of esoteric doctrine have the right to practise it. Rebirth as a demon would be
the punishment that would befall any others who allowed it.

Distinct from the official religion and mystical traditions
of Tibet, there exist many strange practices unsuspected by
the great majority of the Lamas themselves. Borrowed partly
from the Tantrism of the Nepalese and remodelled by Tibetan
occultists, there is absolutely nothing Buddhist, needless to
say, about these practices which are repudiated alike by the
educated Lamas and by the great contemplatives.

Readers who possess some knowledge of the Hindu cult
of Shakti, the Divine Mother with her ten forms (Kâli, Tara,
Rajrajeswari, Bhuvaneshwari, Bairavi, Chinnamastha,
Dhumavati, Balagamukhi, Mathangi, and Mahâlakshmi) will
note a remote analogy between the rite described above and
the *chakra* of the Shaktas who worship this goddess.
Nevertheless, the object of the ritual sexual union is wholly dif-

ferent in these latter from that followed by the Tibetans.

Although somewhat alien to my present subject, I may mention that the Hindu Shaktas hold nocturnal meetings called *chakra* (a circle).

During these meetings, both men and women form a circle, each man seated by the side of a woman. The elements of the cult are *panchatatva* (the five elements) which they designate as the five M's, because the Sanskrit name of each of them begins with this letter. They are: *madya*, wine; *mansa*, meat; *matsya*, fish; *mudra*, dried grain; *maithuna*, sexual union. Certain Hindus affirm that these terms are symbolical and that *maithuna* should be understood as a psychic process having nothing in common with sexual relations. Others say that the rite should be accomplished by the devotee and his legitimate wife, their union thus being raised to the status of a religious act into which no impure thoughts enter. Many Shaktas, however, declare that by those who have attained the loftiest degrees of illumination the wine which has to be drunk at the *chakra* is real wine and the woman with whom one must be united is any woman, *except* one's legitimate wife. As most people, in every country, are ready to form a high opinion of their intelligence and stage of perfection, many consider themselves entitled to the privileges of "those who have attained the loftiest degrees of illumination", consequently the meetings of the Shaktas have often degenerated into licentious orgies. There is nothing of this kind in Tibet.

2

THE VARIOUS KINDS OF INITIATION AND THEIR AIM

Before being entrusted with the rudiments of any *dam ngag* whatsoever, the novice must receive *lung* and one more minor initiation.

The meaning of *lung* is similar to that of *dam ngag*; it is also "advice" or counsel, though of a less solemn nature and not necessarily connected with religious objects, nor always given by a Lama.

No study is begun in Tibet – whether that of grammar or of any science - without the performance of the rite which has received the name of *lung*.

Suppose a young boy wishes to learn the alphabet. On a day reputed by an astrologer or a *ngōnshes*[1] (a seer) to be favourable, he betakes himself to the master whose pupil he would like to become, carrying a *khadag*[2] and a few gifts in accordance with his means.

[1] Written *sngon shes*.
[2] Written *khabtags*. These are silk or muslin scarves. In Tibet these are offered on numerous occasions: whenever one pays a visit, solicits a favour, or leaves a host, etc. They are also offered to the statues in the temples. The quality of the material of which they are made and their length denote the degree of esteem in which he is held to whom the *khadag* is offered, as well as the means

If the Master is a monk, the candidate pupil prostrates himself thrice at his feet. If he is a layman, he contents himself with uncovering his head and politely bowing.

Then he takes his place respectfully before the professor, who is seated higher than himself, on a number of cushions. The master recites a short invocation to the Lord of Science, Jampalyang,[1] after which, with the utmost gravity, he utters in succession the thirty letters of the Tibetan alphabet: *Ka-kha-ga-nga*, and so on.

When this is over, before dismissing the scholar he generally recommends him to repeat several times the formula: *Aum ara ba tsa ma dhi di di di di* . . . and this, according to the Tibetans, causes an increase of mental ability.

As a ceremony is considered indispensable to prepare one for the study of the alphabet, it may readily be seen that higher knowledge is not imparted without serious preliminaries.

Whatever the religious book it is desired to read in order to gain the merits attached to its repetition,[2] *lung* is regarded as an indispensable preparation. As has just been described, the pious layman or inferior monk, after the usual prostrations and offerings, must respectfully listen, with folded hands, to the reading of the book by a Lama.

Omission of this ceremony makes the reading of the work to some extent unlawful; in any case, no good result or

of him who offers it. In Southern and Central Tibet, the *khadags* are white. In Northern Tibet, in the province of Kham and in Mongolia, they are blue. The reason of this is that these countries follow Chinese customs. As white is the colour of mourning in China it is not of good omen.

[1] Written *hjamdpal dbyangs*. He is the Bodhisattva and is called, in Sanskrit, Manjushri.

[2] The Tibetans – with the exception of a very small élite – have the greatest faith in the repetition of the Holy Scriptures, even when the meaning of the words uttered is not understood by the reader.

religious merit can result from such omission.

It frequently happens that the officiating Lama gives no explanation of any kind to his listeners who take their departure without having understood a single word that has been droned in their ears. Moreover, it not infrequently happens that the reader shares their ignorance, but this matters little to the majority of the worshippers.[1]

The simple repetition of the well-known formula *Aum mani padme hum!* requires a preceding *lung*.

The *mani lung*, as it is called, is generally conferred in the following manner:

After prostrations and offerings and the burning of incense, each candidate in turn approaches the officiating Lama, holding his rosary in his hand. The Lama then places the devotee's fingers as well as his own on one of the beads of the rosary, reciting the words: *Aum mani padme hum!* He may continue thus with all the 108 beads or utter the formula once only, for a single bead, leaving the worshipper to continue the recital alone.

Sometimes the pious crowd remains seated in front of the Lama, listening to him as he recites *Aum mani padme hum!* on his own rosary 108 times. Each one present draws the beads of his rosary through his fingers simultaneously with the Lama, muttering the formula with him.

There are also various other methods.

Mani lung and other *lungs* for the use of ordinary people are based on the same principle as the great *angkurs*, of which they are a poor imitation.

---

[1]The written Tibet language does not divide the words as do the European languages. Each syllable is uniformly separated from the following one by a full stop. Many of the inferior clergy can only utter each syllable; they are incapable of grouping the syllables into words and sentences, and still more incapable of understanding the meaning of the sounds they utter.

The ceremony called *lung* by the mystic masters differs from the form just described. With them, it corresponds to the formal admission of a candidate as a disciple to whom the *dam ngag* will gradually be communicated. The rite is supposed to create mystic and psychic bonds between the new disciple and "his Lama" and, beyond the latter, with all the masters who have preceded him as successive representatives of the *lob gyud*. Indeed, it is the adoption of the neophyte into a religious family.

On this occasion, a *kyilkhor* (magic circle) is made, the tutelary deities and the Lamas, spiritual ancestors of the *guru*, are invoked. When the rite is over, or on the following day, instructions are given to the novice on the subject of meditation and psychic training.

After an indeterminate period of probation, an *angkur* may be conferred.

Although we have here to use the word "initiation," it may be noted that the Tibetan term thus translated does not correspond to the usual meaning of initiation. The main idea that we attach to initiation is the revelation of a secret doctrine, admission to the knowledge of certain mysteries, whereas the *angkur* is, above all, the transmission of a power, a force, by a kind of psychic process. The object in view is to communicate to the initiate the capacity to perform some particular act or to practise certain exercises which tend to develop various physical or intellectual faculties.

Sacramental initiations are not peculiar to Lamaism. These are to be found in different forms in all religions. The direct ancestor of the Lamaist *angkur* is the Hindu *abhisheka*. Nevertheless, it seems possible that, prior to the introduction of Tantric Buddhism into Tibet, the Bönpos were already conferring initiations the spirit of which is now found in Lamaist *angkurs*. The Sanskrit term *abhisheka* means "to sprinkle", "to consecrate by unction". It is noteworthy that the Tibetan translators (*lotsawas*), whose renderings are invariably so faithful, have rejected the meaning of consecrating by unction, and have adopted that of giving power: *angkurwa*. Their intention to choose another term is made still more evident by the fact that they have retained the idea of aspersion in *tus solwa* (written *khrus gsolwa*), a purificatory rite altogether different from *angkur*.

The Lamaists distinguish between three categories of teaching, three categories of methods and practices, and three kinds of initiation corresponding thereto: the exoteric, the esoteric, and the mystic.[1] In addition, each of these kinds is in three degrees, the common, the medium, and the superior, while each degree contains several varieties.

The exoteric category comprises a large number of *lungs* and *angkurs*. Many of these latter constitute a sort of ritual presentation of a devotee to some eminent personality of the Lamaist pantheon. Following on this presentation, relations which remind one of those of the Roman patricians with their clients are set up between the powerful being belonging to another world and his faithful servant here below. The effects of his protection most generally sought after are: a life that is prosperous, prolonged and free from illness, and a happy rebirth into a paradise.

The most popular of these initiations is that of the infinitely compassionate Chenrezigs.[2] For students there is also the initiation of Jampalyang which aims at obtaining the gift of a keen intellect.

---

[1] In Tibetan: *tchi, nang,* and *ngags* respectively written *phyi, nang,* and *snags.*
[2] Written *spyan ras gzigs*: "He who sees with piercing vision."

Amongst magicians of an inferior order, certain initiations are conferred that are supposed to place the novice under the guardianship of various demons who protect adepts in sorcery.

Hunters receive a special initiation which makes of them the servants and protégés of certain genii whom they must subsequently honour by offering them some portion of the animals they kill. "Initiates" of this category are said to be under an obligation to hunt on certain fixed days under penalty of being afflicted with maladies by the beings with whom they have contracted an alliance. Some of these days – notably that of the full moon – are given up by Buddhists to meditation on the Doctrine and to the practice of good deeds. The faithful must refrain, even more than usual, from taking the life even of the tiniest insect. The flagrant infraction of the religious law further intensifies the reprobation attaching to hunters in Tibet. All the same, especially amongst the frontier peoples, this reprobation is rather theoretical than practical.

The *angkurs* of Padmasambhâva, of the Dâkinîs, of the Changchub Semspas and divers others may be either semi-esoteric or fully esoteric.

Padmasambhâva is the Buddhist-Tantric magician who preached in Tibet about the eighth century. His *angkur* communicates the spirit of the secret methods.

The *angkur* of the Dâkinîs brings one into relation with the mother-fairies who teach mystic doctrines and magical sciences.

The *angkur* of the Changchub Semspas relates the faithful one to the Lords of Infinite Benevolence – of whom Chenrezigs is the most famous – and enables him to enter, in imitation of themselves, on the path of devotion and the disinterested service of all beings.

In the same category is also to be found the *angkur* of

Dolma[1] and many others too numerous to mention.

Certain initiations include under the same name the three forms: exoteric, esoteric, and mystic. They are conferred in one or other of these forms, in the lower, the medium, or the higher degree, according to the mental level of the candidate.

The various *angkurs* of the *Yidams* belong to one or other of the higher categories: esoteric or mystic, according to the teaching given during and subsequent to the celebration of the rite.

The *Yidam* of the Lamaist has been compared by certain authors to the *Ishta Devatâ* of the Hindus. *Ishta* (the desired one) is the name given in India by a worshipper to the deity whom he has chosen, less as a protector than as the object of his passionate love (*bhakti*). The peculiarity of *bhakti* is that the *bhakta* loves his God for his own sake, without asking for any other favour than to be permitted to love him. In *bhakti*, the element of interest found in the worshipper who relies on being "recompensed" by the God he adores, is wholly absent. One *bhakta* said to me: "My God may fling me into hell and torment me therein if such be his good pleasure, and I shall rejoice in those torments since they will be agreeable to him." According to a Sanskrit phrase, often repeated by *bhaktas*, the devotee should love his God "as an unchaste woman loves her lover," i.e. passionately and madly, without regard for anything else. The Hindu worshipper aims at living with his *Ishta Devatâ* in the future life or entering into mystic union with him. Indeed, the beatitude he envisages – carried on to the spiritual plane – is but that of the loved one uniting with her beloved, without anything further.

This kind of mysticism is totally unknown in Tibet. Here

[1]Generally pronounced *Deuma* and written *sgrolma*. She is the goddess Tara of the Hindu-Tantric pantheon.

the *Yidams* play a very different part from that of the *Ishtas*; their worship gives no occasion for any manifestation of "spiritual sensuality".

According to exoteric theories, the *Yidams* are powerful beings who protect those who reverence them. Esoteric teaching depicts them as occult forces, and mystics regard them as manifestations of the energy inherent in body and mind.

So concise an explanation is, of course, very incomplete.

Any Changchub Semspa may be chosen as Yidam, but when – as often happens – he has two personalities, one benign and the other fearful,[1] it is generally this latter that is preferred as protector. As regards the other mythical characters amongst the *Yidams*, they are of the most terrible type and must not be mistaken for the gods (*lha*).

Certain *Yidams* are even of demoniacal descent, such as Tamdrin, Dza, Yeshes-Gompo, and others.[2] We must, however, guard against attributing to Tibetan names, which for lack of other words we have to translate by the word "demon", the meaning which this term carries with it in Christianity.

As has just been said, initiations of the exoteric category bear the character of a ceremonial presentation to a powerful protector, or of some permission which allows of the legitimate and fruitful performance of a special act of devotion.

The significance of the esoteric *angkurs* is more subtle. They aim at introducing the new initiate into the psychic communion of those who have in the past performed – or are now performing – the rites he is himself about to practise.

The result of this wide-flung communion, say the

---

[1]For instance, the greatest of all the *Yidams*: Dordje Jigsjyed, is the awe-inspiring aspect of Jampalyang, the *Changchub Semspa* who, in Lamaism, is regarded as Lord of science and eloquence. Nagpo Chenpo is the wrathful counterpart of the compassionate Chenrezigs.

[2]Respectively written: *rtangrin, gzah, yeshes mgonpo.*

Lamaist mystics, is to give to the ritual acts performed by the officiating monk and to the magical formulas he utters, a power which a mere novice would be incapable of imparting to them.

Presentation to a superhuman being affects, esoterically, the nature of a partial fusion between the worshipper and the worshipped; the former benefits by participating to some extent in the virtues and the power of the superior being with whom he remains in close contact.

Esoteric *angkurs* are also conferred upon disciples who are beginning certain practices, such as meditation on the mystic centres of the body,[1] *tumo*, the art of warming oneself without fire, or who train themselves by the practice of certain rites such as *chöd*, in which one's body is offered as food for famished demons.[2]

The initiations called "mystical" (*sngags*) are psychic in character. The theory upon which they are based is that the energy emanating from the master, or from more occult sources, may be transmitted to the disciple who is capable of "drawing it off" from the psychic waves into which he is plunged during the celebration of the *angkur* rites.

The Lamas say that at this moment a force is placed within the grasp of the novice. To seize and appropriate it constitutes his part in the ceremony, the success of which depends on his skill.

Consequently, although the initiating Lama supplies the energy which his disciple must assimilate, the latter has anything but a passive rôle to play. In the course of conversations on this subject with initiated mystics, I heard several of them

---

[1]The *khorlos* (written *hkhorlo*) "wheels", also called by Tibetans *padma* (lotus). These are the *chakras* of the Tantric *yogins*.
[2]*Tumo chöd*, etc., are described in detail in *With Mystics and Magicians in Tibet*.

define *angkur* without distinction. The reason of this is easy to understand. No one can supply another with what he does not possess or is incapable of borrowing elsewhere.

If he lacks the particular power which has to be communicated in a certain *angkur*, but remains capable of profound mental concentration, the Lama is able, it is believed, during the celebration of the rite, to attract currents of influence emanating from his own *guru* (even if the latter is dead), from a *Changchub Semspa*, or from a *Yidam* with whom he is in habitual psychic or devout relationship.

The few hermits connected with the *gongs gyud* line confer absolutely silent initiations which are extremely impressive. Here several hours of meditation, during which Master and disciple are seated motionless, in front of each other, take the place of oral instruction.

The object of these Masters is not to impart instruction to their pupils, nor even to suggest subjects for reflection, but rather to develop in them faculties enabling them to come into direct contact with the objects to be known and to discern in them something more than their outer appearance – as is usual with the majority of mankind.

The masters of the *Da gyud* line silently hint at symbolical gestures during the initiations.[1] They also point to different objects, or group them in different ways, in order to awaken ideas in their disciples.

Before the celebration of a mystic *angkur*, the initiating Lama remains in a retreat for a period varying from a few days to several months. The higher the degree of the *angkur* to be conferred, the longer the retreat, as a rule. While it lasts, the *guru* remains in a state of profound concentration, all his

---

[1] The Zen Buddhists of Japan also use gestures in the lessons they give to novices.

thoughts centred upon one point. In mystical phraseology, this is called one-pointedness of mind. Employing a somewhat unusual metaphor, though one that well expresses the object of this practice, I would say that the Lama stores himself with psychic energy, just as an accumulator stores itself with electricity.

The aspirant after initiation also retires from active life and prepares himself, both mentally and physically, to receive the force which will be transferred to him. His religious practices, his food and sleep, are regulated in accordance with the advice of his master. He also endeavours to empty his mind of all reasoning activity and to impose silence upon his physical sensations, so that no mental or physical activity may take place and thus form an obstacle to the stream of energy which is to pour into him.

All this may seem strange and even absurd; nevertheless, the scientific investigation into these processes might possibly lead to interesting discoveries. We are still almost wholly ignorant of psychic forces, and of the various ways in which they may be employed.

The mystic *angkurs* may be classified into two groups. The first includes those that deal with the practices of yoga,[1] the most important of these being breathing exercises. To the second group belong the *angkurs* relating to the practice of introspective meditation and to mental training in general.

Still, this distinction between the studies to which these

---

[1]Yoga is the name of the Hindu philosophical system attributed to Patanjali. As contemplation is highly extolled in yoga, various complicated methods of meditation and psychic training have been elaborated and given the name of yoga, although the original meaning of the word is "union". There are several methods of yoga: hâtha yoga, laya yoga, rajah yoga. The Tibetans translate the Sanskrit term yoga by *naldjor* (written *rnal byor*). This, however, does not mean "union", but "complete mental tranquillity", consequently, "mastery in contemplation".

angkurs serve as introduction, is mainly a theoretical one. A certain degree of skill in the exercises of yoga, principally in the mastery of the art of breathing, is regarded as almost indispensable to success in contemplation.

Very few, it is said, are those who, at will, obtain perfect concentration of thought by purely intellectual means.

In another direction, the methods intended to effect the acquisition of supernormal physical powers, such as the increase of internal heat, lightness of the body, the possibility of effecting rapid marches of extraordinary distances without food or rest, etc. . . . always involve an element of mental training.

For this reason, *angkurs* of both groups are separately conferred on disciples aiming at spiritual liberation; Buddhahood. Those who desire supernormal powers receive a sort of mixed *angkur* generally known as *lung gom kyi angkur*.

Whereas the initiations of the lower degrees sometimes afford occasions for pompous ceremonies, at which several candidates are present, the ritual of the mystic *angkurs* is exceedingly sober in character.

These latter are conferred, without witnesses, in the master's private abode, or in his hermitage if he is an anchorite. In the highest degrees, ritual is almost or wholly absent, and the *gongs gyud* silent method of thought transmission is then practised by certain *gurus* of the contemplative order.

The following description may afford some idea of an esoteric or mystic *angkur* of the lower or middle degree, among the adepts of the "Short Path".

The candidate knocks at the *guru*'s door, asking permission to enter and receive *angkur*. It is sometimes required that he should not have met anyone, or been seen, even from a distance, when proceeding from his abode to that of his Master.

From within, the Lama asks the novice questions

regarding the motives that govern the step he is taking. He warns him of the difficulties and dangers awaiting the traveller along the mystic Path, and advises him to renounce an arduous enterprise that bristles with dangers and to lead a virtuous though easier life.

Yidams, *Dâkinîs* and the symbolical Deity at the head of the sect to which the Master belongs[1] are evoked by him and conjured to guard his door and to prevent the candidate from approaching the secret *kyilkhor* if he is unworthy.

At this moment, certain Lamas raise imprecations against the man who dares to solicit initiation with treacherous or impure mind; they order the *Yidams* and the *Dâkinîs* to manifest under their most frightful forms and to tear the profaner to pieces.

Wild and savage music succeeds the Lama's declamation: drum, tambourine, handbells, cymbals, and *kangling*[2] blend in one common sound. In the less secret ceremonies, when the officiating monk is assisted by disciples who are already initiates, the infernal din produced by the instruments and the Lama's moanings followed by the fierce cries of his acolytes, are well calculated to terrify a credulous novice.

Other Lamas regard all this as vulgar. Their novices should listen attentively in order that they may hear, uttered in low tones, inside the room, sentences whose meaning may be translated somewhat as follows:

"Pass thy way, traveller; stay not here. Many are the pleasant dwellings both in this world and in the others. Live a virtuous life and follow the precepts of the law. Easy and full of charms are the ways that lead to the abodes of bliss.

"Behind this door is a steep and rugged path, enveloped in

---

[1]For instance, Dordje chang in the Dzogschen sect.
[2]*Kangling* (written *rkang-gling*): a trumpet made out of a human thighbone or an ivory imitation thereof, producing a harsh sound which carries far.

gloom. Obstacles, painful to surmount, elusive mirages, exhausting struggles are to be encountered at every step. Is thy foothold sufficiently sure to scale those heights? . . . Art thou bold enough to face any danger, however perilous? . . . Art thou wise enough to have destroyed all illusions? Hast thou overcome attachment to life and dost thou feel capable of kindling within thyself the torch which must shed light upon the path? . . ."

The candidate is also reminded of what he was told when seeking admission as a disciple, that in entering upon the "Short Path" he runs the risk of incurring dangerous illness, of madness and certain happenings of an occult nature that may cause death.

Yidams and *Dâkinîs* are also conjured occasionally, though silently. The impression produced is only the more vivid in consequence.

When the preliminary rites are over, the door is opened and the novice admitted within. On entering, he throws himself at the feet of his master and in front of the *kyilkhor*. The order in which the prostrations take place differs according to the sects and the Lamas.

Many think that the *kyilkhor* in which the *Yidams* and the *Changchub Semspas* momentarily reside, should be adored first, others declare that this opinion only shows the ignorance of those who profess it.

A tradition of the *Kahgyudpas* states that Marpa, the founder of their sect, was blamed by his master Narota for prostrating himself first before the *kyilkhor*.

"It is I who have constructed the *kyilkhor*," declared Narota. "It is I who have instilled into it such life and energy as it possesses. But for me, there would be nothing there but lifeless figures and objects. The deities who inhabit them have been born of my spirit; consequently, it is to me that homage is first due."

It is said that the error committed by Marpa, on this occasion, was the reason why the spiritual line of Narota instead of being continued by his son[1] (Marpa was a married Lama), passed to his disciple Milarespa.

The disciple should enter the room with his eyes downcast. After prostrating himself, he looks at his *guru* and the *kyilkhor* one after the other, fixing his eyes first on the feet of the former and the lower portion of the latter, then gradually raising them until he sees the head of the master and the upper part of the *kyilkhor*.

Afterwards he is permitted to sit down. During certain *angkurs*, the disciple takes his place in the middle of a magic circle.

Each kind of *angkur* has its own special rites and these also vary according to the *dam ngag* into which one is initiated, the sect to which the master belongs, the degree of the *angkur* conferred, whether esoteric or mystical, common, medium, or higher degree, etc. . . .

Holy water, poured into the hollow of the hand, is drunk by the disciple. Consecrated pills may be given to him.[2]

Different symbolical objects such as the vessel containing the "water of immortality", a lighted lamp, a religious book, a reliquary, etc. . . . are placed for a moment upon his head.

After being blindfolded, he is led in front of a metal or wooden plate on which there has been traced, with grain or

[1]Marpa's son Dodebum died when young by an accident. He had gone to a festival with some friends and, on returning home, his horse was startled by the shouts of his companions, who were probably excited by drink as is the custom with Tibetans after a banquet. The animal bolted and Dodebum was flung into a ravine.

[2]These also are inappropriate terms, used for lack of better ones. This water is not "holy" and the pills are not "consecrated". The Lama has kept them close by him for a certain space of time, concentrating his thoughts upon them, and, it is supposed, storing precious energies within them.

coloured powders, a schematic drawing representing the five parts that make up the personality (form, sensation, perception, subjective differentiation, and consciousness) set around a circle which signifies the Void.

The disciple must throw a little arrow on to this drawing. Omens are predicted from the position taken by the arrow when it falls, its point indicating one or other of the five constitutive parts. The most excellent omen is when the arrow-point pierces the circle in the centre. This means that the new initiate will be able to liberate himself from the bonds that constitute each part of the personality, i.e. to attain to Nirvâna.

Certain *angkurs*, preliminaries to modes of training which aim at the acquiring of supernormal faculties, involve strange symbolical gestures which are anything but pleasant for the one who has to perform them. I will confine myself to quoting only one of the less painless of them.

During the initiation which precedes the training intended to develop internal warmth,[1] the neophyte has to swallow a lighted candle. This is made of butter and may attain to a length of four inches. Anyone who is not a professional mountebank and cannot allow himself to juggle it away, finds this little test – I speak from experience – wholly devoid of charm. This same *angkur* is generally conferred in winter, upon the high mountains. The disciple must remain naked during the entire ceremony, i.e. for four or five consecutive hours. In certain cases, and when women are being initiated, a single gown is tolerated.

As a rule, however, the candidate, previous to the day of his initiation, has submitted to so many tests and endured such great suffering that he has become quite adequately hardened.

[1] *Tumo*: See *With Mystics and Magicians in Tibet*.

To be slightly frozen, to burn his mouth and laboriously digest a candle at such a moment seem to him mere trifles.

The *angkurs* relating to the practices of *lung-gom*, to the cult of *Yidams* and deities, to the power of subjugating demons and to magic are not included amongst the gradual initiations which mark the various stages along the mystic Path of the Lamaists.

According to certain Lamas, these mystic *angkurs* that have only spiritual ends in view are five in number. All the same, four would appear to be the orthodox number. Milarespa in his autobiography mentions only four of them, whilst his Master Marpa declares that he himself was acquainted with no more than four.

This, too, is the number of *angkurs* leading to spiritual perfection which the famous Lama, Longchen, mentions in a treatise in my possession.

My personal experience inclines me to believe that the "five" *angkurs* belong to another series of initiations, in which this number has been retained because it corresponds to the five parts whose aggregate, according to Buddhism, constitutes the personality, i.e. form, perception, sensation, mental concepts or subjective differentiation and consciousness.

Nothing could be more complicated or involved than the rites of the Tibetan esoteric schools which exist alongside of official Lamaism. Orientalists interested in these subjects will find a rich field of labour in Tibet.

By the way, I may mention that there are eight progressive initiations among the Hindu Tantrikas.

The spiritual life, as conceived by the Lamas, comprises two great stages, subdivided into many others of less importance. The first is that of "activity", the second that of "inactivity", including simple inactivity and absolute inactivity.

In spite of the lengthy explanations here given concerning initiations, I think special importance should be attached to two initiations in the mystical category, the one "with activity" and the other "without activity". I shall here find an opportunity to enable my readers to be present at secret ceremonies never hitherto witnessed by foreigners.

The account here given of these rites is based on the oral descriptions, given to me by competent Lamas, of what I have seen myself, and also on a ritual, of which I have the text, written by the famous Lama, Longchen, author of several authoritative mystical treatises.

INITIATION "WITH ACTIVITY"

The first of the four *angkurs* that lead the disciple to spiritual maturity is called *spros btchas mtchog gi dbang bskur* (pronounced *teu ches chog gi angkur*), "the excellent *angkur* with activity."

In order to be qualified to confer it, a Lama must be deeply versed in the three sections of the Lamaist canonical Scriptures which deal respectively with philosophical doctrines, ritual, and metaphysics.

The qualifications required of the disciple are as follows:

His feelings towards the Master who is to prepare him for an undimmed contemplation of Reality must be identical with those he would feel for the Buddha himself. He must have faith in him and in the efficacy of the *angkur* he confers.

Note that, in this latter condition, Lamaism is quite distinct from the orthodox Buddhist doctrine which teaches that ten "bonds" prevent human beings from attaining to salvation.

The third of these bonds is, in canonical terminology, "faith in the efficacy of religious rites". According to the teaching of primitive Buddhism, repudiation of the belief in the efficacy of sacramental and other ceremonies is indispensable before the first step can be taken towards spiritual enlightenment. This is technically called "entering the stream".

Nevertheless, when this divergence of views is pointed out to Lamas fully competent in esoteric methods, they reply that the opposition of principles is only apparent and altogether provisional. Rites, they say, have no other effect than that of a sort of physical therapeutics, and the ritual form of certain "initiations" is merely a concession to the intellectual inadequacy of the disciples. The end is to free oneself of all these means. The great contemplatives abandoned them; Milarespa is a famous instance.

There are also those who have never needed to use them. As we shall shortly see, the liturgical words uttered during the mystic initiations confirm the sayings of the Lamas. Indeed, they tend to exhibit to the novice the power and intelligence existing in him in a latent state, to induce him to develop them and rely upon them alone.

The disciple should prepare himself to receive the *angkur* of "activity" by living a pure life, "fleeing from evil actions as one flees from a poisonous serpent". Having observed the absurdity of the motives that impel the masses, and desirous of being bound by the sacred engagements which predispose the mind to form just opinions, the candidate should be ready to offer to his master, as a testimony of his veneration, his entire fortune, his person, and his life.

Care must be taken not to regard this latter condition as mere rhetoric. Naturally, I doubt whether any *guru* has ever made it a condition for the reception of an *angkur* that his disciple should commit suicide or be killed when the ceremony was over. Such things are to be found only in legends. By the way, some of these latter are very fine. Heroic men are stated to be willing to meet death, to be devoured by a demon who knows some important truth, on condition the latter reveals it to them. The saint often requests permission to inscribe the truth upon a rock for the instruction of his fellow-creatures; then he offers himself to the monster. But even when the knowledge he purchases so dearly momentarily benefits himself alone, it must be understood that, from the Buddhist point of view, his sacrifice has not been in vain. The effect of the knowledge he has acquired will appear in a following life. However, as I have said, such things are only legends.

It is nevertheless a real fact that Masters test their disciples by asking for the sacrifice both of person and of property.

Marpa utilised the services of Milarespa for several years, going so far as to compromise his health and almost his life by making him build, unaided, a house which he several times ordered him to demolish utterly and begin to build again after a new plan.

The same Marpa, when his disciple Chösdor had brought to him all his cattle as an offering, forced him to return home (a journey lasting several days) and bring back, on his shoulders, a goat which he had left behind in his stable because it was lame.

These two latter facts are particularly well known in Tibet. Many others are told; indeed, contemporary Lamas still retain a liking for these somewhat harsh practices.

In the West, it is scarcely possible to form any idea of the ascendency exercised over his disciples by the Asiatic religious master. I have said that the Tibetans showed themselves less lavish of exaggerated demonstrations than the Hindus in their testimonies of veneration, and that they could distinguish, in the character of their spiritual guides, between what was admirable and what was not. This does not make it impossible that, at certain moments, sudden fervent impulses should arise in the minds of the disciples. Stirred by enthusiasm, they are then capable of actions which most Occidentals would probably regard as insane.

Proceeding to the initiation ceremony, the Lama begins by drawing a *mandala*. The Sanskrit term *mandala* is used in the Lamaist religious literature; it is equivalent to the Tibetan term *kyilkhor*.[1] The Lama Longchen used it equally with that of *kyilkhor* in the text I consulted. And yet there is a certain difference between the *mandalas* and the *kyilkhors*. The former consist of symbolical figures and offerings to deities. The latter may be animated by the presence of certain beings or forces which the Lama introduces; several *mandalas* may enter into the composition of a single *kyilkhor*.

The *mandala* of "the *angkur* with activity" is square.[2] The length of each of its sides is the same as that between the elbow and the end of the middle finger of the Lama who is drawing it. Its surface should be as smooth as that of a mirror. The drawing is traced with powders of five different colours: white, yellow, green, red, blue.

At each corner of the *mandala* is shown a door, in the middle of which is a blue disc on which figures an eight-petalled lotus.

Four "bars" are traced to enclose the symbolical drawing. Their respective colours are: white to the east, yellow to the south, red to the west, and green to the north. Within this enclosure are arranged different offerings, whilst other figures typify various countries, dwellings, etc.

[1] See on the subject of *kyilkhors*; *With Mystics and Magicians in Tibet*, p. 265.
[2] Strictly speaking, however, *mandala*, as well as *kyilkhor*, signifies something "round".

Another "bar" representing *dordjes* surrounds the whole drawing. At the centre and the four corners are placed five ritual vessels, each bearing the inscription *Aum-A-Hum*. These vessels contain a mixture of pure water and milk into which have been placed five kinds of grains, five kinds of medicinal plants, five kinds of perfumes, the "three whites" (cream, cheese, butter) and the "three sweets" (honey, sugar, treacle). Five arrows, five mirrors, five pieces of rock crystal, five pieces of silk of five different colours, five images of the five mystic Buddhas (the whole in miniature) are attached as ornaments to each of the vessels and five peacock's feathers are placed in each of them.

In a goblet shaped like a human skull (sometimes a genuine human skull mounted on three silver feet) is another preparation (sometimes black tea, sometimes grain brandy) representing the beverage of immortality.

A magic dagger is placed near each of the four doors, four knives with curved blades are driven into the *mandala* between the four bars. Ritual cakes (*tormas*) and various objects required for conferring the *angkur* are again placed on the *mandala*, which is finally surmounted with a dais, and surrounded with *thangkas* (pictures which roll up, like Japanese *kakemonos*).

The ceremony of the *angkur* includes three parts:

1. The Lama blesses both himself and the *mandala*.

2. The disciple is admitted into the room in which are the Lama and the *mandala*.

3. The *angkur* is conferred.

At the outset, the Lama, who is alone, summons the presence of the Buddha in the *mandala*.

We must beware of thinking that it is the historical

Buddha that is here being invoked, or even his soul which would be supposed to have its present abode in some paradise or other. In rites of this kind, the term Buddha signifies esoterically the Knowledge possessed by the Buddhas, the spiritual force existing in them and about to be communicated to the disciple.

In the "*angkur* with activity" this first part of the rite is very brief. No sooner is it over than the candidate is invited to enter the place where the Lama has hitherto remained enclosed. This initiation may be conferred either on one or on more disciples during the same ceremony.

The candidate – or each candidate if there are several – prostrates himself before the Lama and the *mandala*. Then follows a liturgical dialogue between Master and disciple. When several disciples are present, they recite all together their own parts of the dialogue. The following translation will give some idea of what is said:

Disciple. Noble Lama, excellent being, most fortunate am I to approach this great secret; I beseech you to admit me to it.

Lama. Son who has behind thee a past of virtuous deeds, entering into the secret vehicle of my precepts thou shalt obtain the good fruits thereof and thy doubts shall flee away while contemplating the jewel of knowledge.

Answer me, art thou happy to have me for thy master?

Disciple. I am happy.

Lama. The five wisdoms,[1] the Buddha, the Doctrine, and the religious Order exist in thyself. Meditation having brought thee to recognise in thyself their essence, pure of all evil, do

[1]The five wisdoms are: (1) The wisdom of the sphere of existence, that which can recognise the fundamental unity of things notwithstanding the differences in their external aspect; (2) the wisdom which causes works to succeed; (3) "the wisdom which distinguishes" (that which makes clearly known all

thou seek the true refuge; i.e. seek refuge in thyself?

Disciple. Aided by the benevolence of my Lama, may I, in this world darkened by ignorance, make use of the lamp of my own method and discover the wisdom which dwells within me.

After this, the Lama ties a string of five-coloured threads to the candidate's left arm. In the event of a female candidate, the string is attached to the right arm. While tying it, the Lama utters a mystical formula (*snags*).

Then, while reciting other *snags*, he takes up a vessel containing holy water, which lies before him outside the *mandala*, and says:

"This water is the excellent water of the vows that bind. If thou breakest these vows, awful purgatorial fires will burn thee for periods of incommensurable length. If, on the other hand, thou art faithful, thy efforts will be crowned with success. Keeping in thy heart this water, type of sacred engagements, power will rise up within thee." (The power to attain the goal of initiation.)

Then the disciple receives a few drops of water in the hollow of his hand and drinks them.

The Lama, now accompanying his recital with a few infrequent and muffled beats of the ritual tambourine (*damaru*), explains to the disciple the meaning of the so-called "lotus" centres of energy which are located respectively at the navel, the heart, the throat, and the top of the head.

The candidate attentively listens to these explanations.

In order to represent symbolically the fact that wisdom

objects with their particular properties); (4) "the wisdom which equalises" (that which makes known the common characters of things, the identity of their nature); (5) "the mirror-wisdom" (which reflects all things, like a looking-glass, without being affected thereby).

has been veiled by ignorance for a period of time whose beginning can neither be perceived nor imagined, the candidate's
eyes are covered with a bandage of black silk.

Holding in his clasped hands pieces of silk of the five
mystical colours, the candidate says:

"A long sequence of causes and effects from time
immemorial has brought me face to face with the present vehicle of the one eternal light. May I therefore become a member
of this holy family." (The spiritual family formed by the masters and the disciples who have belonged, from its origin, to the
mystic school into which one is being initiated.)

Still blindfolded, the candidate throws a flower upon the
mandala.

At each of the initiations conferred upon him, a new
name is given to the disciple. Here, this name depends on the
part of the *kyilkhor* upon which the flower thrown by the candidate falls.

The following table indicates the names generally given
in this initiation:

Place where the flower has fallen	Men's names	Women's names
In the middle of the *mandala*	Freed from diversity	Infinite extent of space
To the East	Excellent nature	Light illumining space
To the South	Self-born joy	Light of the essence of things
To the West	Blessed king	Lotus upward stretching
To the North	Liberated from the acts of the five senses	Mind extending equally in all directions

The disciple must keep his "initiate" names strictly secret, whereas the name received on entering the religious Order becomes the one by which a monk is subsequently known.

The liturgical recitation continues after the name has been given:

Disciple. Lord, who holdest the sceptre, master most wise, deign to enlighten the ignorance of him who wanders blindly about the three worlds.

Lama. Son of good family,[1] who, blinded by ignorance, has so long sought from without that which is within thyself, with this wand that resembles the jewel Yidjine (the fabulous jewel which grants the satisfaction of all desires) I will enable thee to see the light.

With a golden wand, the Lama removes the piece of black silk which covered the disciple's eyes. At this moment, the disciple must think that his ignorance is dispelled.

Lama. Look, son of good family. Look attentively within thyself; look slowly all around thee. Many things are to be seen.

[1]Son of good family or son of noble ancestors was a classic name already in use during the lifetime of the Buddha. At that time, it applied to disciples who belonged to the Hindu caste of the *Kshatriyas* (nobility) from which the Buddha himself had sprung, to distinguish them from the *Brahmans* (priestly caste). Before the preaching of the Buddha, many nobles vied with the *Brahmans* successfully in the realm of philosophy. In the above-mentioned *angkur*, the name "son of noble ancestors" is used figuratively. It applies (1) to a supposed spiritual ascendancy, the candidate during his previous lives having been adopted as a disciple by masters belonging to a spiritual lineage; (2) to the ascendancy of good deeds resulting in the birth of the candidate as a human being endowed with intelligence and disposed to seek spiritual illumination.

At this point, those of pure mind are said to see the Lama in different aspects, sometimes under the form of a deity or surrounded with rays of light streaming from his body, or again his form having disappeared and being replaced by a "beam of light".

The Lama questions the disciple: "What dost thou see in the *mandala*?" he asks. The candidate names the colour which he sees most particularly of all those used in the drawing of the *mandala*, and this colour denotes the nature of the "wisdom" predominant in him.

Then the Lama successively points with his golden wand to the different parts of the *kyilkhor* (*mandala*), explaining to the disciple the meaning of the drawings and of the various objects placed upon them. Each figure and object is a symbol relating to the cosmogonic theories or to the physiological or psychic constitution of man, as conceived by the Tibetans.

Now we come to the rites for the "transmission of power", i.e. the various *angkurs* which constitute "initiation with activity".

These several *angkurs* are respectively called:

The *angkur* of the mystic master.
The secret *angkur*.
The *angkur* of knowledge and wisdom.
The *angkur* of symbolical words.

1. *ANGKUR* OF THE MYSTIC MASTER

The ritual gesture of this *angkur* consists in touching with the vessels containing holy water the four points of the body where, according to the Lamaists, are the centres of psychic forces, and then in pouring a drop of this water upon each of these places.

As has been said, the five vessels are placed on the *kyilkhor*, one in the middle and each of the others at one of its angles in the direction of the four cardinal points.

The vessels bear the following symbolical names:

Vessel of the sphere of existence.
Vessel of the eternal nature.
Vessel of wisdom upspringing of itself.
Vessel devoid of passions.
Vessel of the wisdom which speedily brings about a state of bliss.

The disciple sits cross-legged, in the usual attitude of the statues of Buddha.

The Lama, taking the vessel which is in the middle of the *kyilkhor*, places it on the candidate's head and says:

"The vessel of the sphere of existence is filled with the precious water of light. Blessed son, now that thou art empowered,[1] thou understandeth the nature of existence."

The mystic language of Tibet is full of imagery, using technical terms for which it is difficult to find equivalents in Occidental language. Here, the "sphere of existence" is also that of the "natural laws". After all, it is a matter of discerning the nature of the material and physic phenomena which make up the world.

The Lama pours a drop of holy water on to the candidate's head. This action signifies that the purification of the

[1] Besides the noun *angkur* the Tibetan language has a verb *angkurwa* (*dbang bskurwa*) that is "to give the power". This is the word used in this passage and is therefore translated "to empower".

centre of energy which mystic theories locate at the top of the head, has taken place.

Lama. This vessel and this water symbolise the wisdom of the Doctrine radiating within the Void.[1]

Blessed son, now that thou art empowered, know the wisdom that comprehends the fundamental unity of all things. May the true knowledge which dwells within thee awake.

The vessel at the east of the *kyilkhor* is placed against the candidate's heart.

Lama. The water that is unimpeded and springs up of itself fills the vessel of "the eternal nature". Blessed son, understand the meaning of the original and fearless basis of things.

A drop of water is poured on the place of the heart,[2] signifying, as above, that the centre of energy at this place has been purified.

Lama. This vessel and this water symbolise self-luminous intelligence unchecked by any obstacle. Blessed son, now that thou art empowered, know the mirror-wisdom.

The mirror-wisdom is that one of the five wisdoms which gives true knowledge of the things reflected in it as in a mirror,

---

[1]This is also explained as the immanent wisdom of things existing in the Void. To understand these expressions, one must be familiar with the various meanings of the term "void" in Mahâyâna Buddhism.

[2]The disciple is wearing his usual costume; he is not naked or covered with a simple cotton robe as is necessary for the other *angkurs*. The drop of holy water is then poured over his garment on the region of the heart and on that of the navel.

and which, like a mirror that remains unchanged, no matter what objects or scenes it reflects, serenely contemplates the action of phenomena.

The vessel at the south of the *kyilkhor* is placed against the candidate's throat.

Lama. The precious water of the desire for Knowledge fills the vessel of "wisdom upspringing of itself". Blessed son, now that thou art empowered, succeed in thy endeavours.

A drop of water is poured on the candidate's throat.

Lama. This vessel and this water symbolises the desired knowledge which, from all eternity, exists in wisdom born of understanding.

Knowing thyself, thou shalt realise thy desires. May the "wisdom that makes all equal" manifest itself within thee!

This technical expression means the wisdom which discerns the identity of nature of all beings. Such wisdom is acquired by contemplative meditation.

The vessel at the west is placed against the candidate's navel.

Lama. The precious water is happiness which ennobles activity fills the vessel that is free from passion. Son, receive the power to become passionless.

A drop of water is poured on the navel. This centre of energy also is purified, as stated above.

Lama. This vessel and this water symbolise eternal spirit, passionless and blissful, which under the form of the flowing water of immortality makes its way through the body's centres of energy (lotuses). "Know the wisdom that discriminates!"

This refers to the wisdom that distinguishes between the particular characteristics of all objects of knowledge and catalogues them correctly.

The vessel at the north is placed in succession at each of the four places touched by the other vessels: the top of the head, the heart, the throat, and the navel.

Lama. The precious water of "activity in security" fills the vessel of the "wisdom which speedily brings about a state of bliss". Blessed son, be empowered with the mighty force that brings the fulfilment of one's purpose.

A drop of water is poured upon each of the four parts of the body above-mentioned for the purification of the centres of energy said to be placed there.

Lama. This water and this vessel symbolise the safe arrival in the eternally free essence, the luminous radiance of spiritual energy.
This self-enlightening, self-liberating, and self-springing wisdom, this great force of an all-perfect eternity, know it as being "wisdom combined with activity".

2. THE SECRET *ANGKUR*

The actions of this rite are the same as those of the *angkur* of the mystic master just described, the only difference being that, instead of touching the candidate's body with vessels filled with holy water, it is a human skull that is placed in succession on the head, the heart, the throat, and the navel. This is done but once. The skull is cut in such fashion that its upper part forms a goblet. The latter is supposed to contain the potion of immortality, symbolised as already stated by grain brandy or black tea.

The liturgical text, considerably shorter than the preceding, refers to the "father and mother" symbol, personifying method and knowledge. It alludes also to the psychic streams of energy circulating through the body and to the exchanges of forces working between the various beings in the universe.

Theories and symbols of Shiva origin predominate in this *angkur* which is far removed from the orthodox Buddhist style.

3. THE *ANGKUR* OF KNOWLEDGE AND WISDOM

This involves no ritual actions of any kind. For these are substituted "mental activities" (*yid kyi phyag rgya* pronounced *yid kyi chag gya*). The Lama's words relate to theories slightly resembling that of the Hindu Vedanta. Here the world of phenomena is said to be unreal, to constitute a sort of sport (Sanskrit: *lila*) in which, unconsciously and involuntarily, the Absolute, indissolubly united with *Mâya* (illusion), is engaged.

Here, the disciple is invited to look upon action as a sport (Tibetan: *rolpa*) in which the mind find its joy, although it knows – and just because it knows – that the deeds it is witnessing are devoid of reality.

The Lama also informs the disciple of certain forms of meditation which he must practise.

4. THE *ANGKUR* OF SYMBOLICAL WORDS

In an extremely picturesque manner the Lama here depicts

certain phases of the contemplation of the sun which he compares with those of the formation of the worlds, as taught by the Lamaists.

"Between heaven and earth, the winds as they cross one another from innumerable whirling *dordjes*": an image representing the aggregation of the atoms.

Then the association of the mind with matter is dealt with in a manner that reminds one of the theories of the Sankya school of philosophy.

Ignorance acting as a force drives the mind to issue from the Void and enter into the "city of the five elements". It is now going to enter the mighty round and pass successively into the kingdoms of the six species of beings, now happy, now unhappy, though deliverance is immediate when the mind has recognised itself; then it escapes from the world in which it was imprisoned, returns into the Void and there seeks repose.

Nevertheless, this is no drama enacted in time, and there is nothing real in these various episodes. The Lamaists regard it as a false conception of our nature, and of that of the world around us.

The highly figurative Oriental tongue imbues these somewhat cloudy theories with a poetic element impossible to express. Here, the bewildered mind is represented as a hero painfully traversing a narrow tortuous pathway, then escaping from a prison, returning home and falling asleep on his couch.

INITIATION "WITHOUT ACTIVITY"

Whereas the preceding *angkur* may be conferred in the abode of a Lama living in a monastery, the rites of "initiation without activity" should be performed in a quiet though pleasant spot.

The *mandala* is twice as extensive as in the preceding rite. I shall not describe it, thus avoiding repetitions that would weary the reader. Suffice to say that the figures and objects that constitute it differ slightly from those employed in "initiation with activity".

The time required for the Lama's preparation is long. He has to perform various rites and meditate for several days. Were he to fail in this, "his words and his mind would not be purified", and he would not be empowered to confer the *angkur*. Like the preceding *angkur*, this, too, may be administered to several disciples during one and the same ceremony.

Immediately before entering the place where the Lama is shut in, the disciple must wash and purify himself with the smoke of sweet-smelling plants. Then, as he noisily clashes cymbals together, he identifies himself with one or another awful deity, imagines himself surrounded by a circle of flames, and finally, holding in his hand a few small sticks of incense, he enters and after prostrating himself before the Lama and the *kyilkhor*, sits down and says:

I have obtained a human body, though difficult to acquire (I was born a man, not a being of another species). I was born in the land of Jambu (literally this is India, but the Tibetans here refer to a land where the Buddhist teaching prevails). I have met with a holy Lama and the great Doctrine. The time has come for me to enter the path of salvation. I now ask that I be initiated into the great Doctrine.

During the long and painful succession of rebirths, like a navigator on a disabled ship in mid-ocean, like a bird caught in a net, like a traveller lost on a dangerous track, like a condemned man in the hands of the executioner, even so would I now liberate myself.

Deliverance is a gentle breeze,[1] calm, bliss devoid of fear.

[1]These texts copy the style of the Indian Buddhist texts which are familiar, in

This initiation also comprises several *angkurs* and two degrees: the vulgar and the non-vulgar.

VULGAR DEGREE

After somewhat lengthy preliminaries, the disciple implores the blessing of the spiritual ancestors of the Lama who is about to initiate him; he praises the Lama and seeks refuge in the Buddha, in his Doctrine and in the religious Order. Then he binds himself by the following vows:

I will never humiliate my co-disciples; I will speak no evil of them.

I will do no harm to animals.

I will not insult men deserving of respect.

I will do no harm to monks.

I will not separate myself from the masters of secret methods.

This very day I renounce all religious rites.

I will be faithful to my vows.

I will use my body, my speech and my mind to the best of my ability.

I will never forsake the Doctrine of the Buddha nor my duties towards my spiritual master.

I will neither betray nor deceive any living being.

From now until the day when I become a Bodhisattva (a highly evolved being who will become a Buddha in a following life), I will do nothing unreasonable.

I will be attentive to the instructions of my spiritual guide.

translation at all events, to all educated Lamas. The "gentle breeze" regarded as delightful in a hot country, would probably have become a "tepid breeze", had the image been of Tibetan origin. Nevertheless, a fresh – not cold – wind is regarded as extremely pleasant by the Tibetans, who cannot tolerate heat.

I will cause no suffering to any being.

I will ask for nothing on the path of beatitude.

I will not conform to the desires of the world, though to do so should cost me my life.

From this day onward, I will have no confidence in cemeteries or in hermitages (as places more suitable than others for practising meditation and obtaining spiritual illumination).

I renounce all worldly occupations.

I will never give up those occupations that are apart from the world (those which tend to spiritual enfranchisement, to liberation from the round of rebirths, such as meditation).

A drop of holy water is poured into the hollow of the candidate's hand, and he drinks it.

Then comes an exhortation from the Lama. The candidate is forbidden to communicate to non-initiates the mystic words and various other details of the *angkur*.

NON-VULGAR DEGREE

At the non-vulgar degree no use is made either of *kyilkhors* or of any ritual objects whatsoever, and the disciple calls for the *angkur* in the following terms:

O Lama, bearer of the sceptre of the Doctrine, I, the son of your heart, desire the *angkur* of the great accomplishment effected without external aid. Explain to me, O Lama, the final *kyilkhor* which is the essence of our mind. Having entered into it, I shall never go forth.

Lama. Happy and excellent son, enlightened mind, who has not yet received the *angkur* of the great accomplishment, I will explain to thee the *kyilkhor* thereof.

Rejecting all ratiocination one frees oneself from the

bonds of this world, one ceases to take and to reject truth that is inferior.

This is one of the fundamental doctrines of the Lamaist mystics. Inferior or approximate truth (*tha ñad* pronounced *tha niet*), is that relating to the world around us, the truth we regard as real, and which is indeed real in the same degree that we ourselves are real. This truth comprises the distinction between good and evil, pleasant and unpleasant, etc., and leads one to grasp certain things and to reject others. He who has risen to the comprehension of superior truth (*ton tampa*) sees beyond these distinctions and attains to serenity.

The flowers which the disciple is about to throw on to the *kyilkhor* are quite as immaterial as this latter. They are called "flowers of knowledge", and the *kyilkhor* is known as "that which has no doors".

The candidate throws away his monastic toga, a symbolical act of renunciation of the works of this world, even the best, such as profession in the religious Order. He raises his hands to his heart and clasps them, fastens his glance upon the heart of the Lama, and master and disciple remain in profound meditation.

Hermits who are contemplatives generally terminate the initiation with this meditation. Other Masters, however, when the meditation is over, again give holy water to the disciple and discourse at length upon various philosophical opinions, such as those dealing with the "self" (or rather the "non-self"), the "four limits,"[1] and many others. These successive discourses form so many *angkurs*.

[1] These "four limits" are (1) birth – cessation; (2) permanence – discontinuity; (3) existence – non-existence; (4) the manifested universe (the phenomenal world) – the Void.

The extremely technical nature of these dissertations prevents them from appearing elsewhere than in a purely Oriental treatise which would enable long commentaries to be made.

It is said that: to be attentive, enlightened, at one's ease (without being "tense" through effort), remaining at peace, without either grasping at or rejecting anything whatsoever, constitutes the "non-vulgar" initiation of "non-activity".

Marvels that have supervened during the celebration of certain *angkurs* are sometimes related, either by people who assert that they have seen them personally or by others who affirm that they have been told of them by those who have had ocular testimony thereof. It is not easy to obtain information on this matter, for the initiates pledge themselves to maintain secrecy regarding all the circumstances accompanying their initiation. They break this promise only on the rarest occasions, when in their opinion some moral advantage on behalf of another will thereby result.

The marvel may refer to the string which the Lama attaches to the candidate's arm. This operation, instead of taking place during the rite of initiation, is often carried out the preceding day. It also frequently happens that blades of grass, an ear of corn, or other small objects, are suspended from the string.

These articles have remained with the Lama during his retreat previous to the initiation, and the Tibetans believe that, by the aid of concentrated thought, he has endowed them with certain properties.

The initiated candidate keeps the string upon him during the night, and the following morning the Lama himself removes it along with the grass, the ear of barley, or whatever had been attached to it. At the same time, his disciple tells him the dreams he has dreamt.

It is said that strange transformations sometimes take place in these objects: their form or colour changes, they increase or diminish in size; they even disappear altogether.

These signs are regarded as indicating the disciple's inmost propensities; they presage his spiritual future.

Certain masters attach to them the utmost importance; they sometimes postpone the ceremony of initiation or even, basing their action on these omens, absolutely decline to confer it.

Notwithstanding this, apparitions constitute the most frequently mentioned prodigies.

If it be admitted, as it is by the Tibetans, that certain persons are able to make their thoughts visible and even tangible by creating a phantom complete in all parts, these phenomena can readily be explained. It is also credible that, at the moment they take place, the attention of those present being concentrated on one and the same idea of personality, this one-pointedness considerably aids in the formation of a vision.

Traditions and legends relate a goodly number of these surprising facts, but for the most part the descriptions are almost identical and there is but little variety in the types of apparitions.

We are indebted to Milarespa for an account of what took place in the house of Marpa, his *guru*, a few days after the latter had admitted him to the highest initiation he was empowered to confer.

Milarespa was soon to take leave of his Master. This was their last mystic meeting: a sort of sacramental banquet[1]

---

[1]In Tibetan, *tshogs hkhor*, a rite somewhat similar to the *ganatchakra* of the Hindu Tantrikas. Still, in current speech, *tshogs hkhor* simply refers to offerings placed upon an altar.

accompanied with rites in honour of the deities and the spiritual ancestors of the officiating Lama.

Dagmedma, Marpa's wife, prepared offerings for the Lamas and the *Yidams*, *tormas* (ritual cakes) for the Dâkinîs and the *Cheu Kyongs*[1] and Marpa's initiated disciples seated themselves before the *kyilkhor*, of which those present form part of this kind of ceremony.

Then Marpa, in the middle of the circle, exhibited various marvels. Milarespa relates that he showed the figures of Kiepa Dordje, of Khorlo Demchog and several other *Yidams*, and finally symbolical objects: handbell, wheel, sword, etc. . . . Then appeared the mystic syllables *Aum-A-Hum* in white, red and blue respectively; also the six-syllabled formula: *Aum-mani-padme-hum!* To finish, the disciples contemplated divers sparkling apparitions.

Note that, with regard to this latter sort of apparition, these silent fireworks, composed of moving images of different luminous colours, are often contemplated by those who follow the *yogin* system of training. It is in this igneous form that the deities show themselves in the *dubthabs* rites of the Lamaists.

What we regard as more interesting than the wonders wrought by Marpa is the declaration which, according to Milarespa, he made to his disciples on this occasion: "All these apparitions are but mirages, magical formations devoid of reality."

A man whom I met in the land of the Ngologs[2] where he was *amchod* (chaplain) of a minor chieftain, told me of a very

---

[1]Written *Chos skyong* "protector of religion", a class of being frequently of demoniacal origin. They have been subjugated by a holy magician and forced to swear to make use of their power to protect Buddhists and Buddhism from their enemies.

[2]Near the sources of the Yellow River.

striking incident which took place, he said, on the occasion of his own initiation.

He happened to be in front of his Master's hermitage, the door of which was shut, as the rite demands. Within, the Lama was droning the liturgical phrases which evoke Heruka, the mighty Lord of the sect of the Dzogchénpas. As he stood waiting outside, he saw a kind of mist slowly exude from the entire surface of the wooden panel which formed the door. After some time, this mist gradually densified and assumed the aspect of a gigantic Heruka, naked, wearing a crown and adorned with necklaces of dead men's heads, as depicted in various books and paintings.

His attitude and glance were stern and forbidding.

The terrified novice had unconsciously stepped back on beginning to glimpse the phantom, but the latter advanced a few steps.

This was more than the poor candidate for initiation could bear. Panic seized him and he began to run madly down the mountain-side, followed by the menacing Heruka, each of whose slow enormous strides outmeasured fifty of his own.

The pursuit did not last long. Incapable, in his distracted mental condition, of choosing the right direction, the fugitive entered a cul-de-sac and was compelled to stop.

Remembering the warnings he had received regarding the occult dangers that await the pilgrim on the "Short Path", he doubted not but that his last hour had come. Strange as it may appear, however, this idea, instead of increasing his terror, annihilated it. Regaining his mental calm, he sat in meditation with crossed legs and downcast eyes.

The chaplain told me that he was far from being a simple beginning in mystic training when this strange adventure befell him, and his views concerning the existence and the essence of deity were by no means those of the masses. Nevertheless, he considered that whatever might be the nature of the present Heruka, at the time he was a formidable power.

His thoughts then turned to the initiation awaiting him. To renounce it from lack of courage would, he imagined, cause him to fall back from the point on the "Path" which he had already attained. Then he would have to be reborn a great number of times, like a man wholly ignorant of spiritual things, before having another opportunity of hearing the precious doctrines preached by a holy master.[1] This prospect frightened him more than did the phantom, more than death itself. He rose, ready to confront anything, and determined to return at once to his Lama.

During the time that he had remained with eyes downcast, he had naturally lost sight of Heruka. On again finding courage to look up, he saw that the phantom had removed himself. His gigantic form now appeared, barring the entrance of the hermitage.

The chaplain told me that he had never been able to understand clearly what happened afterwards. He vaguely remembered certain incidents following one another at lightning speed. Running up, he reached Heruka, walked straight "through him", felt a pain in his brow and found himself inside the hut, at his Master's feet, before the *kyilkhor* all lit up and perfumed with incense.

As may well be imagined, I did not fail to relate this

[1]There is a belief current amongst Buddhists of all sects that birth as a human being endowed with intelligence and the opportunity of hearing the doctrine of the Buddha preached are circumstances rarely encountered during successive lives. When, as a result of divers causes, it is possible for a human being to advance towards enlightenment and he does not take advantage of his opportunity, the natural result of his lack of interest in spiritual things is that he strays away from the path of Deliverance. After falling in this fashion, he must recommence the painful toil capable of bringing back the opportunity he has neglected.

strange fact to several Lamas, asking their opinion about it.

Some were inclined to believe that the phantasmagoric vision was purely subjective. The man, they said, had lost all consciousness of his surroundings and had lived his strange adventure in a sort of trance. As regards the cause of this latter, possibly the Lama had imposed the vision of Heruka on to the mind of his disciple who had added to and embellished it in his own mind. Or maybe the emotion experienced by the novice when approaching initiation had increased the tension of his mind already concentrated on Heruka, and he alone had been the creator of his own vision.

Others, on the contrary, thought that Heruka was a *tulpa*[1] produced by the externalisation, rendered sensible to another, of the Lama's thoughts. Once the phantom formed, the Lama had controlled its movements, or rather his disciple had done this unconsciously, the deeds of the *tulpa* corresponding with the feelings he himself experienced. His terror had determined Heruka's threatening attitude, and because he had fled, the phantom had started in his pursuit.

Here I may state that, according to the Tibetans, our feelings strongly influence the deeds and thoughts of those with whom we come into contact. Both brigand and tiger, they imagine, become bolder if the man who meets them near a wood experiences fear on seeing them, even though he does not manifest this fear by any outward sign. It is the same with all kinds of feelings.

As usual in such cases, each person questioned had some explanation to offer. The explanations, however, given by people who believed in the existence of a real Heruka – a being belonging to another world – would take us too far from our subject. In Tibet, as everywhere in the East, there are many different ways of "believing in the Gods".

[1] Magical creation (written *sprulpa*).

3

WHERE INITIATIONS LEAD. THE DIFFERENT MEANINGS OF *AUM MANI PADME HUM!*

Where do initiations lead? From what has gone before, the reader has come to understand that initiations in Tibet appear as countless portals opening out upon so many different fields of activity.

A very small minority of monks confine themselves only to applying for the four or five mystic initiations conferred by contemplatives. These aspirants after Buddhahood are solitary individuals seldom seen, who rarely occupy the attention of their compatriots, whether monks or laymen.

It is quite different with the numerous initiates into the doctrines and rites – apparently without any great bonds to link them – for which particular *angkurs* are conferred. In this category there are countless Masters, or so-called Masters, some of whom enjoy a worthy reputation which has not always been wholly usurped. Some of these latter are clever spiritual guides, and the ignorant man who has, latent within himself, the possibility of an awakening of his slumbering intellect, will find himself, slowly but surely, being led by them.

The most trivial of initiations may contain philosophical or mystic developments; this may be seen from the various interpretations given to the well-known formula: *Aum mani padme hum!* and the many practices relating thereto.

Laymen travellers and even Orientalists are at times only too ready to declare empty of meaning what they do not immediately understand. Authors very learned in many other more important subjects, even at the present time, translate the word *Aum* by the commonplace exclamation "Ah!" whereas Amen is given as the equivalent of *hum!* No greater mistake could be made.

Aum may signify the three persons of the Hindu trinity: Brahmâ, Vishnu, and Shiva: also the Brahman, "The one without a second", of the Advaita philosophy of the Vedanta. It is the symbol of the inexpressible Absolute, the final word that can be uttered, after which there is nothing but silence. Sri Sankarâcharya calls it "the stay of meditation",[1] and it is declared in the Mandukopanishad[2] that *Aum* is the bow by means of which the individual "self" attains to the universal "That" (*tat*) which can be called neither *being* nor *non*-being.

The Hindus also regard *Aum* as the creative sound which builds up the worlds. When the mystic has become capable of hearing all together the sounds and voices of all beings and things that exist and move, he then perceives the one and only *Aum*. This *Aum* also vibrates in the depths of his inmost "self" and he who knows how to utter it in silence attains to supreme deliverance.

The Tibetans who received *Aum* from India, along with the mantras with which it is associated, would appear never to have had any knowledge of the various meanings it possesses for their neighbours beyond the Himâlaya, nor of the promi-

---

[1] In his commentary of the Mandukopanishad.
[2] "The Pranava is the bow, the Atman is the arrow and the Brahman is said to be the target." Pranava is one name of the syllable *Aum*; *Atman* is the individual "self".

nent place it holds in their philosophies and religions.

Aum is repeated by Lamaists, along with the other words in the Sanskrit formulas, without their attaching to them any special importance, whereas other mystic syllables, such as *hum!* and *phat!* are considered to be very potent, and are widely employed in mystic and magical rites.

Passing to the following words of the formula, *mani padme* means "the jewel in the lotus". Here we seem to find a meaning that is immediately intelligible, and yet the usual Tibetan interpretation takes no account whatsoever of this literal meaning, the majority of devotees being completely ignorant of it.

The latter believe that the mechanical repetition of *Aum mani padme hum!* secures for them a happy birth in *Nub dewa chen*: the Occidental paradise of utmost bliss.

Some, better informed, have learned that each of the six syllables of the formula relates to one of the six classes of animate beings and to one of the mystical colours, as follows:

> *Aum* is white and relates to the gods;
> *Ma* is blue and relates to the non-gods;[1]
> *Ni* is yellow and relates to men;
> *Pad* is green and relates to animals;
> *Me* is red and relates to non-men;[2]
> *Hum* is black and relates to the dwellers
>   in the purgatories.

[1]The *Lha-ma-yin*, a kind of Titans ever at war with the gods of whom they are jealous and of whose dwellings they endeavour to make themselves masters. They are the *âsuras* of Hindu mythology.
[2]These non-men (*mi ma yin*) include the *Yidags* (the *pretas* of Hindu mythology). Their gigantic body resembles a mountain whilst their neck is thread-shaped. The ridiculous amount of food capable of passing down the throat is quite inadequate to feed these monsters who are perpetually

There are different opinions as to the effect of the six syllables upon the beings to whom they correspond. Some say that their repetition helps the latter to evade further rebirths and leads them direct into the Occidental paradise: *Nub dewa chen.*

Others look upon this idea as absurd. The gods, they object, have no need to be led into a Paradise, as they already dwell in one or other of these happy abodes.

As for evading rebirth by entering into *Nub dewa chen*, that also is nonsense. The Buddhist Doctrine expressly teaches that life is transitory in all words whatsoever, and that death is the inevitable end of the beings born into them.

Others again see the effects of the six syllables in another light. It is not, they assert, the beings of the six species that are set free from the circle of rebirths by the repetition of *Aum mani padme hum!* but rather the man who recites the formula that liberates himself from a rebirth in one or other of these worlds. When we have accepted this opinion we have taken a step towards views that are more worthy of our attention.

Many pious Tibetans of both sexes are content to repeat the sacred formula, convinced that it produces its effect of itself, after they have received the initiation which secures for them its fruits.

Nevertheless, there are certain explanations regarding this mysterious process.

Aum mani padme hum! serves as a stay for meditation which may be described somewhat as follows:

The six kinds of beings are identified with the six sylla-

---

tormented by hunger and thirst. When they approach water, it becomes transformed into flame. To assuage the sufferings of these wretched beings, the Lamas every morning offer them holy water to drink. As a result of the rite performed over it, this water does not change into flame when the *Yidags* come to quench their thirst. In the category of the "non-men" are also included the demi-gods, genii, spirits of various kinds, both benevolent and malevolent.

bles which are imagined to be of their respective colours, as indicated above. These latter form an endless chain and, carried on the breath, permeate the body, entering by one nostril and leaving by the other.

In proportion as mental concentration becomes more complete, the chain is mentally seen to lengthen. The syllables, astride the breath, are carried far away with the out-breathing before being again absorbed with the in-breathing. And yet the chain is never broken, it stretches like a rubber band and remains all the time in contact with the one who is meditating.

Gradually also the form of the Tibetan letters becomes transformed and those who "obtain the fruit" of this exercise perceive the six syllables as six worlds in which the innumerable beings belonging to the six species arise, move and sport, suffer and disappear.

Thus it is clearly seen that the six worlds and their denizens are purely subjective: a creation of the mind from which they issue and into which they are reabsorbed.

In the subsequent description of breathing exercises, it will be seen that certain of them consist in holding the breath without expiration and others in not reintroducing air into the body[1] by inspiration immediately following expiration, which is technically called "remaining empty".

In meditation upon *Aum Mani padme hum!* when the six syllables are carried out with the breath, one imagines the birth of the six species of beings that endure so long as the breath "remains out of the body". A new in-breathing brings back the entire phantasmagoria of the universe to the one who meditates. It is absorbed by – and remains in – him so long as he

---

[1] I use the words advisedly "into the body" instead of the usual expression "into the lungs" because Tibetan theories are either ignorant of, or do not take into account, the part played by the lungs.

holds back his breath.

By means of this practice, more advanced mystics enter into a trance in which the letters of the formula, the beings they represent and everything related thereto, are engulfed in "that" which, for want of a term to express it, the Mahâyâna Buddhists have named the Void.

Then, on attaining to this vision and a direct comprehension of the Void, they are set free from the illusion of the world as we conceive it, and, consequently, liberated from the rebirths resulting from this illusion.

We note the resemblance of this theory to that current in India regarding the "days and nights" of Brahmâ, his alternating periods of activity and slumber represented also in Hindu cosmogony by the "breathing" of Brahmâ. According to this doctrine, the Universe is put forth when Brahmâ out-breathes and returns to him when he in-breathes.

"When day comes, all phenomena issue from the unmanifest (*aviakta*). When night comes, they are reabsorbed into it."[1]

"All beings return into my material nature (*prakriti*) at the end of a kalpa. At the beginning of the following kalpa, I again send them forth."[2]

In the meditation here described, the Tibetans substitute themselves for the hypothetical Brahmâ and think: the phenomena I sense proceed from the creative might of my mind; they are a projection without of that which exists within it.

This does not signify that there does not exist "anything" objective, but only that the phenomenal world, *as we see it*, is a fantastic mirage, a materialisation of the forms we conceive.

As the present work does not deal with the study of

---

[1] *Bhagavad Gîta*, VIII, 18.
[2] *Ibid.*, IX, 7.

Tibetan philosophy, instead of proceeding farther in this direction we will examine another of the many interpretations of *Aum mani padme hum!*

This interpretation does not take into account the division into six syllables but examines the formula as regards its literal meaning "a jewel in a lotus", these words being looked upon as symbolical.

The simplest interpretation is: in the lotus (the world) there exists a jewel (the doctrine of the Buddha).

Another interpretation regards the "lotus" as typifying the "mind", in whose depths introspective meditation brings forth knowledge, truth, reality, deliverance, Nirvâna, these various terms being different names of one and the same thing.

We have now obtained a meaning related to one of the most striking doctrines of the Mahâyâna Buddhists, that in which they differ from their co-religionists, the Theravadins (followers of the Hînayâna).

In accordance with this doctrine, Nirvâna, the final salvation, is by no means wholly distinct from and opposed to the world of phenomena (*samsâra*). Mystics discover the former in the heart of the latter. Nirvâna (the jewel) exists when enlightenment exists. Samsâra (the lotus) exists when there is ignorance-illusion which veils Nirvâna, just as the lotus with its many petals covers the jewel hidden amongst them.[1]

Hum! at the end of the formula is a mystical expression denoting anger. It is used in rites whose object it is to subjugate demons and awe-inspiring deities. How does it happen to have been added on to the "jewel in the lotus" and to *Aum*, the sacred syllable of the Hindus? This, too, is explained in various ways.

[1] I have used the Sanskrit terms *Nirvâna* and *samsâra* because they are so well known. The Tibetans say *korwa* (the round) for *samsâra* and *tharpa* (deliverance) for Nirvâna.

Hum! is a kind of mystic war-cry, shouted out to defy the enemy. Who or what is the enemy here? Some regard it as evil-working demons, others as the trinity of evil propensities which keep us in the circle of rebirths: lust, hatred, and stupidity. More subtle thinkers consider the enemy to be the imaginary "self" that we hold so dear.

It is also said that *Hum!* signifies the mind free of all ideas concerning objective things.

A seventh syllable is added to the formula to terminate it, after a number of repetitions, generally one hundred and eight, as that is the number of beads in the Tibetan rosary. Lamas versed in the secret language teach that this syllable, *Hrî*, indicates the profound reality hidden beneath appearances, the fundamental essence of things.

Whereas the ordinary devotee will confine himself to the initiation (*lung*) described in the preceding pages and to the mechanical repetition of the well-known formula, other devotees, during higher initiations, will gradually have imparted to them its various esoteric and mystical meanings.

DUBTHABS RITES

A considerable number of *angkurs* (initiations) are connected with the so-called *dubthabs* rites which hold an important place in Lamaistic practices.

The term *dubthabs* (written *sgrub thabs*) signifies a "means or method of success". The objects to which these methods are said to lead are divided into four:

1. Gentle or pacific (*shiwa*) for obtaining a long life, health, good fortune.
2. Expanding (*gyaispa*) for obtaining wealth and fame.
3. Potent (*wangwa*) for obtaining influence and power.

4. Terrible (*tagpo*)[1] for obtaining the power to cause evil, to kill or destroy in whatsoever manner, by occult methods.

How can these different results be attained? Some answer that they are the work of deities who grant their aid to those who reverence them in the required manner. Others affirm that the aim of the *dubthabs* is not to worship the deities but rather to bring them into subjection; they also say that the man who is versed in their ritual is capable of forcing both gods and demons to place their power at his service and to obey him in everything.

These opinions are current in Tibet, but both of them, according to more learned Lamas, denote a lack of understanding of the theories on which the *dubthabs* are based.

In reality, judging by the explanations we find in the works of ancient authors and those given orally by contemporary masters of mysticism, the method employed consists in projecting, like images on a screen, deities mentally conceived and in imagining a series of changes through which they pass, in the course of very prolonged and complicated rites.

The beings evoked by the *dubpapo*[2] are not imaginary creations of any kind, they are always well-known personalities in the world of gods or demons, who have been revered or propitiated for centuries by millions of believers.

Tibetan occultists say that these beings have acquired a sort of real existence due to the countless thoughts that have been concentrated upon them.[3]

---

[1]Written respectively: *shiwa*, *rhyaspa*, *dbangwa*, and *dragpo*.
[2]He who celebrates the *dubthabs* rite.
[3]The Tibetans insist strongly upon this point. I have given instances of it several times in *With Mystics and Magicians in Tibet*. See more especially p. 147. See also the French edition of *L'Inde hier, aujourd'hui, demain.* p. 19 *et seq.*

Similar theories are expressed in the Sacred Scriptures of India. In the *Brihad Aranyakopanishad*, 1, 4, 10, which is regarded as prior to Buddhism, we find these words: "Whosoever worships a deity with the thought in his mind: 'He is another, another am I', does not know; like a beast, he is *used* by the gods. As verily many beasts maintain a man, so every man maintains the gods."

How do men do this? By feeding the subjective personalities of their gods on the worship they pay them, a Hindu ascetic told me.

Enlightened Lamas are fully aware of the nature of the characters they evoke, but they assert that, by this kind of mystic sport, it is possible to obtain results which could never, or only with great difficulty, have been obtained otherwise. What is the explanation of this oddity?

The Tibetans say that when, during the celebration of a rite, the thought of him who officiates becomes concentrated on the deities, these latter, who "already exist", become to him even more real and powerful. In identifying himself with them, the *dubpapo* places himself in communication with an accumulation of energy vastly superior to what he could produce by his own efforts.

Contact with this mysterious power may prove beneficial to him who celebrates the rite, procuring for him the satisfaction of his desires. Nevertheless, if he is lacking in skill – mainly in the *dubthabs* of the "terrible" category – he may be ill-treated and even killed by the mighty personalities that his mental concentration has attracted.

The mystics of Tibet consider that gods and demons, paradise and hell, exist only for those who believe in them. Although existing in a latent state, the god created and kept alive by the imagination of the masses has power only over the man who comes into contact with him. A filament is necessary in order that the electricity dormant in a storage battery may cause the light to appear in the lamp. This comparison explains with a fair degree of accuracy what is in the minds of the Tibetans.

The majority of the *dubpapos* are not aware of the dual origin of the deities – whom they revere during the ritual ceremonies. They do not comprehend that the latter are born of the mental concentration of the masses of believers and, again, temporarily created by the thought of him who acts as a magnet attracting these already existing occult forces or personalities. Many of them believe that the only object of these ceremonies is to impress the mind by the sight of beings possessed of a real objective existence and objectively visible in their divers abodes. This impression must, in their opinion, bring into close contact the *dubpapo* and the deities he has honoured.

Those who succeed in comprehending the subjective nature of the deities evoked during the *dubthabs* are advised by the masters not to regard these deities as negligible phantoms. It is said in the *dubthabs* of Pal Khorlo Demchog that mentally created deities are similar to those supposed to inhabit Paradise and other sacred places. In the very words of the Tibetan text, "They should be regarded as the two-faced unity which appears as form and is, in essence, the formless Void".

He who officiates should also conceive of the different deities in the divers parts of his body and understand that they all exist in himself. The better to fix this idea in the minds of those who practise the *dubthabs*, most of the latter end by causing to re-enter the body of the officiating monk, and to be absorbed therein, the gods and demons that have been projected by him.

The best way to give a somewhat clear idea of these rites, so different from any practised in the West, is to summarise one of them. The main lines of procedure are practically identical, whatever be the personality evoked during the *dubthabs*.

The one I now take as a model is the *dubthabs* of Dordje Jigsjyed, the grand *Yidam* of the sect of the "Yellow Caps".[1]

In a perfectly shut room, where the *dubpapo* runs no risk of being either seen or disturbed, he seats himself in front of a picture of Dordje Jigsjyed. The celebration of the rite requires what are technically called the "seven members" of the service (*yenlag bdum*). i.e. (1) prostrations; (2) offerings to the deities; (3) ransom for sins committed; (4) to welcome virtuous inspirations; (5) to wish that the doctrine of the Buddha be preached; (6) to beseech the saints not to enter Nirvâna – with the result that they remain in the world to help their fellow-beings; (7) to apply all accumulated merits to the acquiring of Buddhahood.

Lamps and *tormas*[2] are placed in front of the image of Jigsjyed. Before the officiant on a small table are placed a handbell, a *dordje*, a human skull used as a goblet, a *damaru*.[3]

The *dubpapo* begins by chanting a long litany, consisting of the names of various personalities, some mystic, others historical. Each group of four names is followed by the invocation: "Grant me, I beseech you, the fulfilment of my desire."

The different categories of the ends aimed at have just been mentioned. The *dubpapo* indicates the precise object he desires. For instance: May I be appointed governor of such or such a province. May I prosper in my business. May I win my lawsuit. May I be loved by such or such a woman. May I live long. May my enemy die. Certain mystic *dubthabs* are also per-

---

[1] The title of the ritual I am following in my description is: *dpal rdorje bjigs byed kyi sgrubthabs*.
[2] Ritual cakes shaped like a pyramid.
[3] A small drum held in the hand.

formed to obtain spiritual advantages. Though he may not speak his wish aloud, the *dubpapo* must always have it in his mind when uttering the liturgical phrase: "Grant me the fulfil-ment of my desire."

Then the creative process begins. The officiant imagines that Dordje Jigsjyed leaps out of his body. The *Yidam* pos-sesses a single face and two hands,[1] one of which hold a curved knife[2] and the other a skull-goblet. His spouse embraces him in the special ritual posture of the *Yab-Yum* (father and mother).

The *dubpapo* must remember that the *Yidam* represents method and his spouse knowledge. She entwines the *Yab* because method and knowledge are an indivisible pair. Whatever kind of success be aspired after, it can be obtained only by the union of the two.

The *dordje* and the handbell symbolise the same idea. In his right hand the officiant holds the *dordje*. In his left he holds the handbell which he tinkles as he recites:

"The *dordje* is method, the handbell is knowledge; both are the true essence of the fully purified mind."

The liturgy continues, interspersed with philosophical declarations on the essentially empty nature of all things.[3]

Offerings are made to Jigsjyed, consisting of flowers, incense, lamps, water, food, music, but all these things exist simply in imagination and are each represented by a special gesture.

---

[1] In some of his many forms this *Yidam* has several heads and countless arms.
[2] A ritual instrument shaped somewhat like a sickle.
[3] This means that all formation is an aggregate of unstable elements, and is devoid of *ego*. Some add a second idea: the Absolute is devoid of all the quali-ties we are capable of imagining, qualities which would limit it. It is nothing that can be conceived by the human mind.

The *Yidam* is created anew; again and again, it is surrounded by different companions and their attitudes, the objects in their hands all have a symbolic meaning.

The *dubpapo* has to meditate long on this symbology until the symbols die away and he sees, face to face, the very things they represent, i.e. he becomes aware of the various kinds of energy that produce the phenomena.

The celebration of the simplest *dubthabs* requires three or four hours; the rite must be repeated for several successive days. Prolonged preparation is needed for the celebration of the grand *dubthabs*, with the requisite initiation by a Lama possessed of the necessary powers. One must also learn by heart whole volumes of liturgical offices, and have an exact knowledge of the ceremonial, the different meditations dealing with the necessary phases of the rite, etc. The rite must be repeated until the *dubpapo* has mastered its exoteric, esoteric, and mystical significations, and has in addition seen manifest signs that augur success.

A strange rite, mentioned in different works dealing with the *dubthabs*, concerns the preparation of the *nangchöd*.[1] Be it said at once that all the ingredients enumerated are imagined, as also is the skull which is not the real skull placed on the table of the officiant.

The process is described as follows in the *dubthabs* of Jigsjyed, of Demtchog,[2] and of others:

From the Void proceeds the syllable *Yam*[3] and from this

[1]Written *nang mtchod*.
[2]The *dubthabs* of Jigsjyed is one of the sect of the "Yellow Caps"; that of Demtchog is more especially practised by the sects of the "Red Caps". They are almost identical.
[3]Yam is the "seed" of air or wind; *Ram* that of fire. It is impossible to translate these mystical terms. Originally they represented sounds which, uttered

syllable comes the blue circle of air. Above is the syllable *Ram* and the red circle of fire. Still higher is the letter A, the primordial sound. From this A emerge three human heads forming a tripod on which is set a white skull "as vast as endless space".

Five kinds of meat, each symbolised by a syllable and coming from the different cardinal points, enter into the skull: from the east comes ox meat; from the south, dog meat; from the west, elephant meat; and from the north, horse meat. The centre supplies human flesh. From intermediate points, such as the north-east, etc., come the impure products of the body: blood, urine, etc.

To the imagination of the officiant, each of these ingredients appears not in its real aspect but as letters and syllables.

Above the skull[1] the *dubpapo* imagines the syllable *Aum* as white, the syllable A as red, and the syllable *Hum* as blue. From each of the three syllables springs a ray of light; these rays come together and fire is kindled to heat the meats and other substances that are in the skull. Boiling makes them liquid. The liquid thus obtained is regarded by some as *dutsi*, the "potion of immortality", and by others as the Elixir of Knowledge "which bestows enlightenment".

This description has led certain authors[2] to imagine that

with the correct intonation (the desired number of vibrations, as one would say in modern scientific terminology), were considered to be creative. The Lamaists have retained these syllables, though they rather use them by making their form objective. I have indicated this point in *With Mystics and Magicians in Tibet*, p. 221.

[1]This must be mentally pictured as a skull cut in the goblet form, like those from which the ascetic *naldjorpas*, the adepts of the "Short Path", drink. They sometimes line these gruesome goblets with silver and add a gold lid and support representing three human heads which symbolise the past, the present, and the future.

[2]See Jaeschke in his *Tibetan-English Dictionary*, under the word *nangmchod*.

some beverage of this kind was actually drunk by pious Tibetans at the celebration of their usual rites. This is quite incorrect. Lamas from whom I have sought information on this point have told me that, in any case, one of the meats needed for the preparation of this "soup" was not to be found in Tibet – elephant meat.

Nevertheless, as *dubthabs* are of Hindu and Nepalese origin, it is possible that the extraordinary "soup" that has become symbolical in Tibet may really have been prepared elsewhere. The depths of absurdity into which superstition has dragged man would seem impossible to fathom.

GYMNASTICS OF RESPIRATION: *GURU* STORIES

I have already said that certain initiations are related to training in the control of the breath.

This kind of gymnastics, unknown in the West, has been practised in India from time immemorial. During the lifetime of the Buddha, 2,500 years ago, it was very popular, and the Brahmains of that period taught many exercises for acquiring almost absolute mastery over inspiration and expiration.

What is the object of these exercises? It would be easier to say what is not their object. Treatises on yoga describe hundreds of them, dealing with all kinds of objects, material and spiritual. Some are intended to lead to the development of the intellect, to mental illumination; others to endow the senses with a supernormal keenness or to bring new faculties into being; others again are to prevent indigestion, to make the voice harmonious, to attract the love of all women, or to permit a man, making himself voluntarily cataleptic, to allow himself to be buried alive and to return to life a few weeks later. Free play has been given to the most extravagant fancy in describing these wonderful effects, and others even more curious.

The favour accorded to these practices by the peoples of India has been in no wise diminished by the passing of the centuries. There are few Hindus who do not indulge in them daily, at all events in the restricted form of holding the breath during the hasty repetition of a formula at the morning devotion; numerous are those who beg clandestinely for instruction in the practices.

Gurus are not lacking. While the Hindu is quick to become a disciple, he is almost equally ready to dub himself a master. The ingenuity he shows in both these rôles is often amusing. I have seen many instances of this, and will now quote two.

One evening, in Calcutta, where I was staying with friends, in the native quarters, I saw through a window two men seated facing each other, with crossed legs, in a shed in front of my dwelling. One of them wore nothing but an eyeglass; the other, quite a youth, was dressed in the most Edenic simplicity.

The man with the eyeglass was the *guru*; he was giving his attentive pupil a lesson on breathing exercises. I saw him stop his nostrils, breathe out violently or slowly, and hold his breath, indicating, with an air of superiority, the swelling of the veins on neck and temple.

After various acrobatic tricks, master and pupil with crossed feet began to leap about like frogs, each one kicking his own posterior with his heels. The former had removed his eyeglass. He now held it in his hand, like a conductor wielding his baton, and, while beating time, encouraged the novice with voice and gesture.

The scene was lighted by a candle fixed in the ground, and the lesson lasted until it had burnt out.

One morning, a few days later, I saw a native, correctly dressed in European fashion, coming from the house opposite.

I was immediately attracted by his face, for he wore an eye-glass. I recognised the nude *guru*, and wondered what profession he exercised when dressed in ordinary clothes. On making inquiry, I discovered that he was a salesman in a drapery establishment.

On another occasion, when living in Benares, a man dressed as a *sannyâsin* (ascetic), advanced through the garden to the balcony where I happened to be.

"Madam, would you kindly give me eight annas (half a rupee)?" he said, in perfect English.

His attitude was not that of a beggar; he expressed himself politely, but not humbly. He had himself fixed the amount of the alms for which he asked, and now, calmly fastening his eyes upon me, he awaited my reply.

"You do not look at all like a beggar, *swamiji*,"[1] I said, "You seem to be a thorough gentleman. I am well aware that a *sannyâsin* must beg for his food, but this ancient custom is now very seldom followed by respectable members of your Order."

"I graduated at an English university," he replied. "Returning to my own country, plague broke out; my father, mother, and wife are all dead. Despair took possession of me; I asked to be ordained as a *sannyâsin* and immediately started on my wanderings. I reached here last night. . . ."

The tragic story told me by this man might well be true. Plague had recently caused many deaths even at Benares.

"What can you do with eight annas?" I asked. "I will gladly give you a few rupees for your more pressing needs."

"Thank you," answered my interlocutor. "Eight annas will prove amply sufficient for today. Tomorrow I shall no longer require help."

---

[1] Lord; the title given to *sannyâsins* when addressing them.

I insisted, but to no purpose. Going down into the garden, I handed him the coin for which he had asked. With a polite bow, he took his leave.

Three days after this incident, I went to the tomb of the famous ascetic Bashkarânanda, which I occasionally visited in memory of the old saint whose pupil I had been in my youth. When close to the spot, I came across a group of people with my *sannyâsin*-gentleman at the head. On the face of his followers I recognised that expression of intense fervour peculiar to Hindu disciples accompanying their Master.

He advanced in tranquil assurance. The bamboo, with its threefold knot and a salmon-coloured muslin bow, symbol of renunciation of the three worlds,[1] held aloft in his thin brown hand, resembled a shepherd's crook. He recognised me, smiled unobtrusively and with an almost imperceptible gesture pointed with his beribboned staff to his small flock of devotees.

You see, the gestures signified, I am now a *guru*, and my faithful disciples – who will increase in numbers – will provide for my every want. Your eight annas were quite sufficient.

Was the man an imposter? Doubtless not so much as many other "Masters". He was learned, and, I am sure of it, capable of lecturing on many a philosophical theory. It may be that, while teaching them to others, he himself became drawn powerfully to the great Hindu doctrines, to the fascinating ascetic life on the banks of the Ganges, and that he became as enthusiastic as any of his disciples. India is the land of the most amazing prodigies.

---

[1]Renunciation of the present world, of the world of one's ancestors – i.e. of posthumous glory – and of the world of the gods (Paradise). One class of *sannyâsins* include this symbolic staff in their religious outfit, always carrying it about with them.

So long as improvised *gurus* are content to discuss philosophical ideas, it is only the pupil's brain that is imperilled. When they become professors of physical exercises the danger extends to the health of the body.

This is especially the case as regards the gymnastics of breathing. All kinds of accidents befall those who adopt such practices inconsiderately: blood-spitting, ruptured ear-drums, and various other troubles.

While it is good to regulate the natural functions of the body, it is absurd to do violence to them. No genuine master of mysticism ever recommends his disciples to take up practices that might prove harmful.

Indeed, breathing exercises which, when practised in places where the air is perfectly pure, may be hygienic, are nothing but a method invented for procuring mental calm.

The Buddha who had rejected the physical practices of the Brahmans – after thoroughly experimenting in them – did not attach any great importance to breathing exercises in his spiritual method, perhaps he had even completely discarded them. The use of some of these practices by Buddhists may be due to his disciples who returned to them after the death of the Master. As the Buddha never wrote anything himself, and as the traditions regarding his discourses only appeared in writing long after his death, we can know nothing definite on this matter.

However it be, the canonical Scriptures of primitive Buddhism simply mention "the consideration of in- and out-breathing" as a way of cultivating attentiveness, and naturally such exercises fall within the scope of practices in mental training.

We may give as an example the so-called "contemplation of the body", one of the "four fundamental attentivenesses". This practice is described as follows:

"The pupil retires into the forest, to the foot of a tree or some other lonely spot; there he seats himself cross-legged, body erect, and attentive, concentrated mind.

"First he breathes in, then he breathes out. Whilst taking a long breath, he is conscious of it and thinks: 'I take a long inhalation.' Similarly, when he takes a short inhalation, he knows it. When he takes long or short exhalations, he is conscious of them.

"He thinks: 'I am about to breathe in,' or, 'I am about to breathe out,' and he acts accordingly, training himself to calm and to master this physical function."

To what does this practice lead? The commentary of a Buddhist monk[1] well versed in the orthodox traditions of the Theravadins, explains it as follows:

"After the disciple has, through contemplation and in- and out-breathing attained the four trances[2] he reflects upon the basis of breath and he understands that in- and out-breathing presuppose the existence of a body. The 'body' is but a name given to the sum of the four main elements and to the properties attached to them, that is to say, the eye, the ear, the nose, the tongue, body, form, sound, smell, taste, etc. Occasioned by contact of the senses and their respective objects, consciousness arises and through consciousness arise the five aspects of existence: the mental aspect formed by perceptions, sensations, subjective formations, consciousness and material aspect, that is to say form.

---

[1]Nyanatiloka. He was a German Buddhist who died in Colombo on 28 May, 1957. He was born in Wiesbaden on 19 February 1878 and founded a hermitage on a small island near Dodanduwa in Ceylon where he lived with his disciples. He was a personal friend of the authoress.

[2]Here is a description of these four trances as it is given in the Buddhist scriptures: The first trance is exempt from envy, anger, sloth, and anxious thought while there are present reasoning, reflection, rapture, happiness and concentration of the spirit. After the suppression of all ratiocination, but retaining rapture and happiness, the disciple attains inward peace and the unification

"The four foundations of attention, that is to say, contemplation of the body, of the sensations, of thoughts and of subjective phenomena, make perfect the 'seven elements of illumination' which are, attention, search for and examination of truth, energy, interest, concentration of thought, and calmness of spirit. And, in their turn, these seven elements produce wisdom and deliverance."[1]

Learned Lamas are acquainted with these theories, but, in this connection, the practice of breathing exercises is of but the faintest interest to them.

With the exception of a few meditations, such as those on *Aum mani padme hum!* described above, in which the going and coming of the breath serves as a basis of mystic contemplation, breathing gymnastics, amongst the Lamaists, aim generally at the obtaining of physical results.

The first thing asked of the man who wishes to train in accordance with one or another of the methods that aim at sporting exploits is the complete mastery of breathing. To acquire it, the following exercises are recommended:[2]

Breathe in slowly through the right nostril, and breathe out slowly through the left nostril.

Breathe in slowly through the left nostril, and breathe out slowly through the right nostril.

---

of the spirit that is born of concentration. This is the second trance. After the suppression of rapture, the disciple remains in a state of calmness of spirit while keeping his senses keen, he is of clear consciousness and he feels in his heart the sentiment of which the sages say "Happy lives the man whose spirit is calm and meditative". This is the third trance. When the disciple has thrown away both pleasure and suffering and has abandoned the earlier joys and pains, he enters into a state of serenity void of pleasure and pain, into the neutral and clear-seeing state which is that of the fourth trance or ecstasy.
[1] In Buddhist phraseology, "Deliverance" is salvation.
[2] As regards these breathing exercises, Tibetans on the whole do not look at things in such detail as do the Hindus, and the most respected masters confine themselves to teaching only a few.

Breathe in slowly through the right nostril, and breathe out rapidly and forcibly through the left nostril.

The same exercise in the reverse direction.

Breathe in rapidly through one nostril, and breathe out rapidly through the other: do the reverse exercise. Breathe in and out, at first rapidly, then slowly through the same nostril.

Breathe in through both nostrils at once: then breathe out in the same way.

Hold the breath. With considerable practice, this can be done without breathing out, for a very long time.

Beginners often reckon the length of the time spent in holding the breath, by touching in succession with the finger-tips, the forehead, then each knee, and then snapping the fingers. Each time they snap the fingers they count one, then two, then three, etc.

Or again, the beginner mentally repeats a formula and with the aid of a rosary counts the number of times he has repeated it whilst holding his breath.

Just as one holds one's breath without exhaling, so one must also learn to exhale without inhaling immediately afterwards, to "remain empty" as it is technically called.

One must also be able to cut short the breathing-in before the end of the inhalation has been reached and to breathe out the air already inhaled. The contrary exercise should also be done: to cut short the breathing-out before the end of the exhalation, and breathe in.

One must learn to breathe in extremely slowly and then to breathe out at the same rate, either by the nostrils or by the mouth, pressing together the lips so as to leave between them an opening no larger than a pin's head. Contrariwise, one must breathe in forcibly, immediately introducing a considerable quantity of air into the lungs, which must then be emptied by expelling this air violently through the nostrils. This exercise causes a noise resembling that made by a blacksmith's bellows.

Many other things have also to be learned, such as breathing superficially "to the depth of the throat", as the Tibetans say, then to the nerve centre which they consider to be in the middle of the chest near the upper part of the stomach, then "to the navel". Some of them also practise breathing the air by way of the rectum and cause it to proceed upwards through the intestines; they also indulge in other odd practices, during which the breathing exercises are combined with various extraordinary postures.

4

DAILY SPIRITUAL EXERCISES

Whether he is still a mere novice or certain initiations have already been conferred upon him, the disciple of Tibetan Masters daily goes through different practices in accordance with a programme drawn up by the Lama whom he has chosen to be his spiritual guide. Only those who have reached the end of the path, having gone through the various stages of initiation, are regarded as liberated from these observances. It does not follow that all the disciples, then, renounce them wholly, but they become free to adopt the rule which, they think, suits them, and to modify it at their pleasure. Indeed, most of the mystics – either members of a monastery or anchorites – draw up for their personal use a sort of "routine", assigning particular moments of day or night to divers spiritual practices. Those who have abandoned the aid of this discipline are almost all hermits, absorbed in continual mystic contemplation which is not interrupted by their actions in daily life.

The practices recommended to disciples differ largely. They depend on the character of the novice, on his intelligence, his abilities and spiritual needs, even on his physical constitution. They also depend on the *dam nag* (traditional esoteric teaching) which he follows in his training, and more especially on the personal ideas of his Master as to the respective efficacy of the various exercises.

One must be careful not to consider these latter from the Western point of view. They were not devised for the use of Europeans or Americans whose mental heredity, mode of thinking and of envisaging things, are very different from those of the Asiatics.

As an example, I will summarise a programme of exercises intended for initiated disciples, in a *dam nag lana med pa*.[1]

It comprises four periods known as *thune*, reserved for meditation: the first at sunrise, the second at noon, the third at twilight, the fourth before retiring to sleep.

We will examine them in succession.

I. At sunrise. – Theme of meditation: How does the chain of causes and effects, which constitutes the world, and Nirvâna, which is its beyond, arise both from the Void?

II. At noon. – The theme of meditation consists of three enigmatical phrases similar to those held in honour amongst the Chinese and Japanese disciples of Bodhidharma (the sects of Ts'an and Zen).

> My body is like a mountain.
> My eyes are like the ocean.
> My mind is like the sky.

The disciple receives no indication as to the use he has to make of these three phrases. It is said that they may suggest reflec-

---

[1]Written *blana med pa*, literally "there exist no higher". These are the doctrines of *ati anuttara yoga* professed by the Dzogschen sect.

tions, lead him to states of mental concentration bordering on ecstasy, or enable him to apprehend certain aspects of Reality.

Is so much, then, concealed beneath these strange comparisons? This is asserted by some, and to deny it *a priori* without having made the test in the same environment as Tibetan disciples and without undergoing the preparation prescribed to them would perhaps be a rash proceeding.

While the nature of the ecstatic states produced by these three phrases remains the secret of those who have made the test, it is not impossible to discover what reflections they induce in beginners. The following are a few of these reflections which I have received from young novices with the permission – and in the presence – of their spiritual guides. I will endeavour to translate them as correctly as possible into a Western tongue.

MY BODY IS LIKE A MOUNTAIN

"The mountain is battered by the tempest; my body is battered by the whirl of outer activities. As the mountain remains impassive and steady in the midst of the storm, so my body 'closing the gates of the senses' can refrain from reacting in reflex manifestations of activity, when perceptions and sensations assail it like a hurricane," says one disciple.

"The mountain lends its soil to the forest which thrusts its roots therein. Countless plants feed upon the mountain. . . . It is a symbol of charity, of the gift of oneself," thinks another disciple.

"Detachment . . ." says a third. "Seasons follow one another, covering the mountain with a mantle of verdure or snow; it bears them with like indifference."

The Masters smile; all this is but petty reasoning to which no attention must be paid.

Another explains: "Rising from the vast earth, forming one with it, being the earth itself, the mountain should not be regarded as something separate. All forms – including my own body – spring from the common basis of all things (*Kungji*) and remain attached thereto. They are nothing else than *Kungji*."[1]

The Master again smiles. I feel greatly inclined to say that this pupil may be on the right scent, but the Lama has already spoken: "Meditate, it is not theories that must be found. One must see and realise. . . ."

A young monk declares: "The ocean reflects the light of sun and moon, the moving shadows cast by the clouds, a host of images. These touch but the surface, not one penetrates into the depths. In like manner, the image of the objects which my eyes reflect ought not to affect my mind."

The Master remarks: "This is excellent as a discipline, but more is needed than simply the framing of rules of conduct for oneself. Meditate! . . ."

Another answers his co-disciple, speaking slowly in the faraway voice of one in a dream: "If the ocean," he says, "were to imbibe all the images that stamp themselves on its surface, having absorbed them all, none could any longer disturb the purity of its clear surface. By allowing to sink into the depths of the mind the images reflected by the eyes, until all forms are drowned therein and their shadows no longer trouble the sight, we can see beyond them."

The Master remains silent; he looks upon the disciples

[1]The literal translation of *Kungji* is "the base or cause of everything." Tibetans use this expression to translate the Sanskrit term: *âlaya vijñâna*, "the seat or abode of consciousness", which some regard as "the Universal Consciousness". *Kungji* is rather "the Universal Substances", but Tibetans refuse to determine the nature of this "base of everything". They call it the Void, to indicate the absence of all qualities it is possible for us to conceive. It is really the unknowable Absolute.

seated at his feet.

None answer his mute invitation. Do those who remain silent understand the enigma better than the two novices who have spoken? – I feel that these latter are yet far from having solved the problem.

MY MIND IS LIKE THE SKY

"In the immense void of the sky," was said to me on another occasion, "clouds arise. They come from nowhere and they go nowhere. Nowhere exists a storehouse of clouds. They arise in the empty spaces of heaven and dissolve therein, like thoughts in the human mind."

This speaker departs from the doctrine of primitive Buddhism, which does not recognise the existence of a "mind" different from thoughts, a sort of receptacle for the elaboration of mental processes. I venture to reply after the fashion of the learned Lamas, by quoting a text from the canonical Scriptures, but this unseasonable display of erudition brings me a gentle rebuke.

"Controversy is in its place at the *cheura*,"[1] said the Lama. "Here it is not a matter of repeating the words or opinions of another. Knowledge is coming into personal contact."

This disciple, like his predecessors, is sent back to his meditations.

Meditation on the three phases just considered is succeeded by another along the following lines:

"I lay aside the past:[2] all that I have been or done, my

[1]Written *tchos grav*, a school attached to the college of philosophy in the great monasteries whose students periodically meet for practice in discussion.
[2]The Tibetan term *yugpa* (*hdjugpa*) signifies, to depose, to lay aside, to dispose of.

loves and my hatreds, my griefs, and my joys.

"I lay aside the future: plans, desires, hopes, fears, etc."

There remains the impermanent aggregate which makes up my "self" at this very moment. I examine it, analysing each of its parts.

Whence comes this sensation? Where will it go when it ceases? Whence comes this idea? Where will it go when it ceases?

The same investigation is applied to each one of the five elements which, according to the Buddhists, make up the personality, namely: form, perceptions, sensations, mental formations, and consciousness.

The goal of these introspective inquiries is to lead the disciple to ascertain himself that the elements of the so-called "self" are all impermanent, that it is impossible to attribute a primal origin to this perpetually moving procession of sensations, perceptions, and ideas, or to give fixed form to any of them, all being devoid of substantial reality, of "self".

Continuing in this way, the disciple approaches the comprehension of that one of the eighteen forms of Void recognised by the Lamas which is called *rang djin tong-pa-gnid*,[1] "void in itself".

And so meditation returns to its starting-point. "All is void", and in this Void, the phenomena constituting the universe, the so-called *personality* and the so-called *existence* come into being of themselves.

III. At sunset one observes the going and coming of the breath and practises various breathing gymnastics. Thought is once more directed to the apparent opposition between the Void and the phenomena. Breathing out, one thinks:

[1]Written *rang bshin stongspa gnid*.

"Ignorance arises, it exists." Breathing in, one thinks: "It does not exist; it melts away into the Void." Then, breathing out afresh, one thinks: "Knowledge arises; it exists," followed, after breathing in, by the thought: "It does not exist, it melts away into the Void."

An exercise related to this latter is practised when walking by the Buddhist monks of Burma and Ceylon. As they advance a step, they think: "mind and body are born", and at the following step, "they have disappeared". And so on. The formula is often murmured, either in Pali or in the language of the place, the better to fix the attention. The aim of the practice is to impress upon the mind the fact of universal impermanency, of continual change and becoming.

IV. When the disciple is about to sleep, he lies down in the "lion posture" as it is called, i.e. on his right side, his head resting on the palm of the right hand.[1]

The contemplation prescribed is as follows:

The novice imagines that in his heart there is an octagonal crystal vase containing a lotus with petals of the five mystic colours: white, red, blue, green, yellow. In the centre of the lotus stands the letter *A*, large in size and outlined in streaks of dazzling light.

He imagines another letter, white in colour, on the top of his head. From this letter emerge countless small white *A*'s which rush like a torrent towards the luminous *A* in the crystal vase, pass through it and return to the *A* on the head, forming an endless chain.

Another *A*, red in colour (some say of a brownish red), is

[1]Hindu ascetics and Buddhist monks sleep in this position, and generally without a pillow.

imagined as being in the region of the perineum. From it emerges a stream of little *A*'s in the same colour; these rise towards the luminous *A* imagined in the heart and return to the red *A* which sent them forth, encircling the lower part of the body, as the white *A*'s encircle the upper part.

When attention weakens and sleep overcomes the disciple, he checks both processes and absorbs all the *A*'s into the central *A*. The latter buries itself in the lotus which closes up its petals. Then a stream of light bursts from the flower. At this moment, the disciple must have in mind the thought: "All is empty."

He then loses consciousness of his surroundings. The idea of the room and the house in which he is, that of the world, that of his "self", all completely vanish

Should he wake during the night, the *naljorpa* must hold the thought of "light", the vision of "light", to the exclusion of all else and without introducing the slightest idea of "form".

The most important result of this exercise is to prepare the mind for the understanding of the Void.

A more ordinary result presents three degrees. In the higher, one no longer dreams. In the middle degree, when one dreams, one is aware that events and actions are taking place in the dream state. In the lower degree, the only dreams are pleasant ones.

Be it noted in passing that certain persons assert that the dreamer awakes when he suspects himself of dreaming, or rather that the semi-conscious state which enables him to know that he is dreaming, marks the approach of his awakening. This is by no means the case with those trained in the practice of introspective meditation.

Naljorpas who have not yet attained sufficient peace of mind to sleep habitually without dreaming, are fully aware in their dreams that they are asleep and are contemplating images devoid of reality.

And so it happens that, without awakening, they indulge in reflections on the objects of their dreams. Sometimes they contemplate, as though it were a theatrical performance, the sequence of adventures through which they live in sleep, and I have heard it said that some occasionally hesitate to commit, in their dreams, deeds which they would not like to commit when awake and decide to trample their scruples under foot because they *know* that the deed would not be a real one.

Tibetans hold no monopoly in casuistry of this kind. If I may permit myself a slight digression, I will relate the strange way in which a lady took me into her confidence with regard to a dream which, a few centuries earlier, might have brought her to the stake.

This lady had dreamed of the devil. Surprising to relate, the devil was in love with her. He offered to press her in his arms and an abominable temptation took possession of the sleeper. Being a devout Catholic, the idea of yielding to the temptation filled her with horror, and yet she was urged on by an ever-increasing sensual curiosity. The love of Satan! What depths of voluptuousness, unknown to a chaste spouse, might it not reveal! . . . What an extraordinary experience! Nevertheless, the religious feelings were on the point of triumphing in this struggle when a sudden light flashed through the mind of the sleeping lady. She understood that it was all a dream. And since it was only a dream. . . .

I do not know if my young devotee confessed her "sin" and what her father confessor said about it, but it is a fact that the Lamas show no indulgence whatsoever towards sins committed in like circumstances. According to them, the mental repercussion of an act, whether good or evil, done in a dream, is identical with that which the same act would produce in the waking state. I shall return to this point.

At this period of his training, the novice may sleep all night without awaking to meditate at midnight, as do the more advanced ascetics. He must, however, be awake at dawn, or preferably a little before daybreak.

His first thought must be for the *A* in his heart.

There are two methods of proceeding: the more ordinary one, used by beginners, consists in seeing the *A* escape from the heart and remain suspended in the air. It is contemplated as a symbol of the Void and an effort is made to obtain perfect concentration of thought upon it.

In the second method, for the use of more advanced students, the *A* immediately leaps into space and disappears, as though absorbed by the infinite. Then the disciple remains absorbed in the thought of the Void.

When the sun rises, meditation is continued with the exercise described above under Section I.

So condensed an abridgement as the present one fails to do justice to these practices, setting forth, as it does, nothing but their strange, even puerile, aspect.

I am anything but qualified to defend them, nevertheless it is but strictly honest for me to declare that, considered in the light of a competent Lama's explanations, they assume quite another look.

For instance, the *A* in question is not a simple letter of the alphabet, rather is it the symbol of indestructibility, of existence without either beginning or end, of universal law. By concentrating his attention upon the letters flowing like the water of a river, the disciple finally conceives the idea of streams of energy flowing through himself, the idea of continual and mutual exchanges between himself and the outer world, the idea of the unity of that universal activity which produces here a man, there a tree, farther away a pebble, and a great many other ideas also, say those who practise these exercises.

The idea of a void, linked on to these various practices, relates to the permanent non-compound "self", whose existence is denied in all beings and things, according to the fundamental doctrine of Buddhism as expressed in Tibetan by the words *kanzag dag med pa, tchos dag med pa,* the person is empty of "self" – all things are empty of "self".

This is a translation of the orthodox Buddhist formula: all aggregates are impermanent; all aggregates are painful – all things are empty of "self" (*Dhammapada*).

The Lamaists have specially insisted on this doctrine of the not-self by dividing the third article into two. They say that at a lower degree of illumination, one perceives that his own person is a whirl of constantly changing formations, but the idea is retained of the "self" existing elsewhere. The understanding that all existence is alike *void* of "self" indicates a fuller illumination.

The daily exercises here vaguely outlined and other similar ones are calculated to attract and fix the attention of the beginner, although he does not immediately grasp their meaning or object.

The meditation described under number II aims at producing equanimity. It is hoped that its practise will enable the disciple to reach down into the depths of himself, a region of perfect calm from which he will be able to consider dispassionately his actions, feelings and thoughts.

HOW TO SLEEP AND TO UTILISE THE TIME GIVEN TO SLEEP. HOW TO CONDUCT ONESELF IN THE DREAM STATE FOR DISCERNING ONE'S LATENT TENDENCIES

The Gelugspas or so-called "yellow cap" Lamas, disciples of Tsong Khapa, show less inclination for a life of contemplation than do their colleagues of the "red caps". Most of the hermits living in solitude belong to one or another of the great red sects, the Karmapas, the Sakyapas, or the Dzogchenpas. The Gelugspas who wish to live in retirement mostly content themselves with occupying one of those huts called *tsams khang* (abodes of meditation) built apart, though not far from a monastery, or else to join a colony of *ritödpas* (hermits) whose individual dwellings are grouped together in desert spots.

Richer Gelugspas have residencies in quiet places where they may stay when they desire to isolate themselves.

Their meditations are as a rule less strange and complicated than those of the mystics called *naljorpas*. Still, it must not be imagined that they confine themselves simply to intellectual meditation. On the contrary, many "reds" admit that the varied exercises they practise are only crutches to aid their mental infirmity to progress along the spiritual path until all rites are laid aside, whilst most of the "yellows" seem to look upon ritualism as essential and show greater hesitation in repudiating it.

The most highly advanced among them in psychic training insist on the utility of retaining self-control, even during sleep. In this respect they follow Tsong Khapa, who devotes to this subject several pages of his great work, the Lamrim.

I will now give the main elements of this practice.

Tsong Khapa says that it is important not to waste the time given up to sleep either by becoming as inert as a stone or allowing the mind to sink into incoherent, absurd or harmful dreams.

The disorderly manifestations of mental activity to which one abandons oneself in dreaming entail a waste of energy which might well have been put to some useful purpose. In addition, one's acts and thoughts when dreaming are identical in their results with acts and thoughts in the waking state. Thus it is fitting not to "work evil" when asleep.

I have already pointed out that the Lamas profess this theory, and here we shall find it advocated by one of the most illustrious of them. It will astonish many Westerners. How, they will ask, can an imaginary act have the same result as a real act? Must that man be put in prison who dreamt that he stole a traveller's purse?

The comparison is not a good one; it does not correspond with the Lamaists' point of view. With them it is not a question of "prison" or of a "judge" condemning the thief.

Belief in retribution of good and evil by a personal conscious Power is non-existent among the Tibetans. Even in the popular religious conceptions, the rôle of Shinje, the Judge of the Dead, consists simply in applying inflexible laws which he did not make and can in no way revise. Moreover, Tsong Khapa and his disciples are not here dealing with the common flock of devotees. According to their teaching, the most serious consequences of a thought or an act consist in the psychic modifications which they produce in the individual who is their author.

The material act brings on the doer visible material consequences that are more or less pleasant or unpleasant, but the mental act that preceded it (i.e. the will to do the material act) debases or ameliorates its author in some invisible manner, creates in him occult affinities and tendencies which are profitable or disastrous to him, and this intimate change in the individual's character may also, in its turn, bring about material results.

The Tibetans attach considerable importance to the domain of the subconscious – though naturally they do not call it by this name. They believe that the manifestations of our real nature are impeded by the constraint in which we always find ourselves when awake. The cause of this constraint is that we are then aware of our social condition, our environment, the teachings and the examples which memory brings before us, and countless other things. The secret of this real nature is to be found in impulses which spring from no consideration based on these data. Sleep, largely abolishing these latter, frees the mind from the shackles in which it is held during the waking state and allows the natural impulses freer play.

It is therefore the real individual who acts in dreams, and his acts, though imaginary from the point of view of the man who is awake, are very real *qua* volition, and involve all the consequences attaching thereto.

Relying on these ideas, the Masters of mysticism recommend the attentive observation of the conduct displayed in the dream state if one would arrive at self-knowledge. They are, however, careful to advise the disciple to try to discover how far the waking state is capable of influencing the dreamer's consciousness.

In a word, the opinion of Tibetan mystics is that intention is equivalent to deed. The murderer becomes a murderer the very moment he had made up his mind to commit his crime. Though something should subsequently happen to prevent him from perpetrating it, this in no way changes the psychic state of the criminal.

If this theory be admitted, it follows that a murder committed in a dream denotes criminal tendencies which the constraint of various influences working upon the dreamer alone keeps in check when he is awake. And, as above stated, all the consequences of the mental formation (*duje*)[1] which constitute the will to "kill", result mechanically therefrom.

Tibetans are not ignorant of the fact that dreams may be produced by real circumstances determining in the sleeper sensations which he transposes, when dreaming, into phantasmagorical visions. For instance, a man who is cold when falling asleep may dream that he is camping out in the snow with his companions. But if during the same dream, either by trickery or by force, he steals a quilt or mantle from one of his companions, and wraps it around his body to warm himself, there are certainly selfish tendencies in him.

In Tibet, as in all other countries, there are those who believe in premonitory dreams, though the learned Lamas do not encourage superstition on the subject. The dreams of the great majority of men, they say, spring from a disordered imagination during sleep. The only indications they can deduce therefrom are those that concern secret tendencies of character, as has been stated.

A very small number of *naljorpas*, who have acquired special psychic faculties, sometimes have premonitory dreams, or perhaps learn, in the dream state, facts taking place far away. But this mysterious information is for the most part received by them during a special kind of trance when the subject is neither asleep nor necessarily plunged in meditation. Sometimes the warning assumes the form of symbolical subjective apparitions.

The manner in which one endeavours to become "a *naljorpa* who does not sleep", is given to us as follows:

"When the time to sleep has come, go outside, wash your feet and then lie down in the 'lion' position on the right side, legs outstretched and the left foot lying on the right foot.

[1]Written *hdu byed*.

"Then acquire the perception of light, perfectly grasping all the characteristics of clearness. If the *naljorpa* is impregnated with this latter when falling asleep, his mind will not be enveloped in darkness during his repose.

"Call to memory the teaching of the Buddha. Meditate thereon down to the very moment of yielding to slumber; be very careful to repel any depraved ideas which may arise within you. Acting in this fashion, the time spent asleep will not differ from what it would have been had you been awake. Unconsciously your mind will continue the mental processes towards which you have directed it and, though asleep, you will be practising virtue."

It is also fitting to keep active the "consciousness of awaking". The body being overcome by slumber, the mind should nevertheless remain lucid and watchful. "Your sleep should be as light as that of a wild beast. Then you will be able to awake at the very moment you have fixed upon."

CONTEMPLATION OF SUN AND SKY

The contemplation of the sun and that of the sky may also form part of a hermit's daily exercises.

He fixes his eyes on the sun, forcing himself not to wink. At first he sees a number of dancing points, caused by the dazzling lights, but after a time a single dark point remains. When this latter has become perfectly motionless, he regards his mind as "fixed" and capable of entering upon real meditation. Between the initial dazzling stage, however, and the moment when the one point is "fixed", a whole fairy vision may unfold itself. Slender threads form countless designs, various personages appear. Each of these apparitions is explained and depicted in illustrated treatises which deal with this kind of contemplation.

Other disciples are recommended to contemplate the sky, sometimes to confine themselves to this one practice to the exclusion of all others. In this latter case, they should set up their hermitage in some spot that overlooks a vast extent of bare and uninhabited country, where nothing appears on the horizon to break the uniformity. Some lie on their backs and contemplate the vault of heaven, thus preventing mountains or other objects from breaking in upon their field of vision. This practice is supposed to lead to the first of the "formless" ecstasies, relating to the perception of "the infinitude of space".

This recumbent posture and contemplation of the heavens are supposed to bring about an indescribable sense of union with the universe.

A Lama once said to me: "Just as we need a mirror to see our face, so we can make use of the heavens to see therein the reflection of our mind."

Another anchorite expressed himself in somewhat similar terms. He explained to me that the sky is used as a mirror. In it appears the image of the Buddha, the reflection of the Knowledge and the Wisdom hidden within ourselves. As we are not aware of their existence, the heaven-mirror serves to reveal it to us. The beginner at first thinks he is seeing a vision and receiving an external revelation, but subsequently he understands that he has been contemplating a projection of his own mind. Then he may cease looking at the sky, for he sees the heavens and the entire universe within himself, as an incessantly repeated creation of his own mind.

A strange practice – which has nothing to do with my present subject though I mention it because of its peculiarity – consists in reading on the vault of heaven predictions concerning one's state of health or the approach of death.

This is mentioned in one of the works of the Lama Yang Tig, entitled *The Death-proving Mirror*, and has been described to me orally in somewhat similar terms.

Very early in the morning or about evening, when the sky is very clear, the disciple must stand outside, naked and with arms and legs extended, holding a staff or a rosary in his hand. In this posture he looks "with eyes and mind" (*sic*) into the heart of his shadow. Gazing upon it with the utmost attention, he distinguishes a pale blue light. When this light is clearly perceived, he raises his eyes and looks at the sky. If he distinctly sees, as in a mirror, his complete image, with his four limbs and the staff or rosary in his hand, then he is in perfect health. An indistinct image shows that his health is precarious. If he does not see his reflection at all in the sky, then he is drawing near to his end.

5

THE DALAI LAMAS

Many readers are probably wondering why the Dalai Lama has not yet been mentioned in the present book. As this deals exclusively with Lamaic initiations, it appears to them that the Dalai Lama ought to occupy the most important place in it, as grand master of the initiates. We will now examine this question.

Although Tibet is beginning to be better known and a number of serious books on the country have been published, foreigners are still very ill-informed regarding the Dalai Lama and the part he plays. The best-informed authors – British officials who have either come into personal contact with the Dalai Lama or have kept up diplomatic relations with his delegates – have described little more than the political personality of the ruler of Tibet, this being all that interested their readers.

Apart from these writers, men who not only had never set foot on Tibetan soil but possessed no reliable information as to its inhabitants, have indulged in fables utterly without foundation. Some represented the Dalai Lama as one who understood and spoke every language on earth. Others peremptorily asserted that he was the "pope" of the Buddhists. Others again, spoke of him as a magician usually engaged in working miracles of the most fantastic nature, while some imagined his palace of Potala to be a kind of "holy of holies", inaccessible to the profane and peopled with supermen, hierophants, guardians of dreaded mysteries.

All this is pure fancy. The Dalai Lama is pre-eminently a temporal sovereign: the autocrat-monarch of Tibet.[1]

In *With Mystics and Magicians in Tibet*, I have given a sketch of the Dalai Lama in his rôle as avatar (*tulku*) of Chenrezigs. Here I will complete the details already given in order to avoid misunderstandings as regards this very lofty personage in the Lamaist world.

The Dalai Lamas are the successors of the original Grand Lamas of the "yellow caps" sect. To become acquainted with their history, we must go back to the foundation of this sect by Tsong Khapa, i.e. to the fifteenth century.

The cradle of the Dalai Lamas is the monastery of Gahlden, about twelve miles distant from Lhasa. It was built by Tsong Khapa in a spot contrasting strangely with the sites generally chosen for the erection of *gompas* (monasteries). These, in their proud and somewhat austere solitude, are generally perched on a height; Gahlden, however, is enveloped by a circle of mountains. Two other monasteries, dating from the same period and founded by the disciples of Tsong Khapa, also disdain the peaks and extend over the plain at their feet, but these are quite visible to the passers-by, whereas Gahlden is so completely hidden in a wide funnel-shaped cavity that it is quite possible for the traveller to journey along neighbouring

---

[1]Absolute ruler in name though never so in fact. Powerful ministers have generally directed the conduct of the Dalai Lamas. After the British expedition to Lhasa in 1905, the Dalai Lama had to submit to British influence while now that Tibet has been, as an "autonomous" province, incorporated into the Chinese People's Republic, the effective power of the Dalai Lama has still further decreased.

paths without entertaining the slightest suspicion that a great monastic edifice is close by.

A tradition explains this peculiarity. It is said that Tsong Khapa foresaw that a time would come when his doctrine would be attacked and overthrown in Tibet, and so he wished to provide for the monks, his disciples, a quiet spot where they might take refuge and preserve his teachings for the benefit of future generations.

Tsong Khapa was the first abbot of Gahlden, and it was there that he ended his days. A splendid mausoleum of solid silver and gold, adorned with precious stones and surrounded with a kind of tent, was erected to him in a large temple built in the centre of the monastery. Numerous pilgrims – of whom I happened to have been one – visit this tomb before which hundreds of lamps are continually burning.

Tsong Khapa was simply a religious master. Continuing the work tentatively begun by Atisa and his disciple Domtön (written Bromston), he did his best to reform the very lax monastic disciples of the Tibetan clergy. For this reason, his disciples were called *gelugspas* (*dgelugspa*), "those who have virtuous habits". The name of yellow caps was given to them because Tsong Khapa, doubtless to distinguish them from the other monks who wore red, imposed on them a yellow head-dress. Still, this simple reason did not appear satisfactory to people enamoured of the marvellous.

It is said that a female deity named Dordje Naldjorma appeared to him and advised him to change the colour and shape of his disciples' head-dress, assuring him that, if they wore yellow caps, they would triumph over their rivals, the "red caps".

Abridging the familiar names of "yellow caps" and "red caps" into the shorter form of "yellow" sect and "red" sect, certain foreigners imagine that some Lamaist monks wore yellow gowns and others red ones. I have already stated that this is not so. The monastic costume is of a dark garnet colour, and the shape is the same for all sects and both sexes. The monks of the most important branch of the adepts of the ancient religion of the indigenous Tibetans, the white Böns, have also adopted the same dress. Only the shape of the head-dress, its colour and that of the mantle – a sort of dalmatic called *dagam* (*zlagam*) which the Lamas wear during the services – make it possible to recognise the sects to which those who wear them respectively belong.

We are wrong if we imagine that Tsong Khapa aimed at bringing Lamaism back to the doctrine of the original Buddhism by eliminating accretions of Hindu-Tantric and Bön-Shamanist origin.

He was quite as ritualistic as the former "red caps", and adhered to the greater part of their superstitions. The essential points – one might almost say the only ones – of his reform dealt with monastic discipline. Whereas the "red caps" allow the drinking of fermented liquor and exact celibacy only from monks who have received the major ordination (that of *gelong*),[1] Tsong Khapa forbade marriage and the use of fermented drink to all members of the clergy without distinction.[2]

A religious Master venerated by a great number of disciples, Tsong Khapa was never the infallible head of a Church. Neither his nephew Khasdub Dje (Khasgrub je) who succeeded him, nor the other Lamas who were supposed to be reincarnations of this latter and were abbots of Gahlden in succession, were invested with the power to impose beliefs on the faithful or to excommunicate those whose views differed from

---

[1] Written *dgeslong*, literally "virtuous-mendicant".
[2] It is well known that Buddhism forbids the use of fermented liquors to all its adherents, both lay and religious. Lamaism is very lax on this point.

Alexandra David-Neel

The Lama Yongden

Alexandra David-Neel and her adopted son,
the Lama Yongden, in travelling dress in Tibet

The present Dalai Lama

Lhassa: the Dalai Lama's palace. A feast day procession
is walking round the Potala Hill

Alexandra David-Neel's hermitage in Tibet, about
13,000 feet above sea level

Above A Tibetan anchorite who lives naked
among the snowy mountains
Below A Tibetan initiate performing a *dubthab* rite
in the forest. In his hands are a tambourine,
and a trumpet made from a human femur

Left　The altar of a Lamaist temple
Right　Statue of *Chenrezigs* in a Lamaist temple

their own. That is a prerogative that has never been granted to anyone amongst the Buddhists.

Notwithstanding the intellectual decline of some of them who fell back into superstition, the spirit of the original teaching is still alive amongst Buddhists and powerful enough to prevent the learned clergy from renouncing freedom of examination, so strongly enjoined upon his disciples by the Buddha.

The uncompromising attitude taken up by primitive Buddhists on this point may be seen in a number of passages from the Pali Scriptures. I will quote one from the Kalâma sutta.

Some young men made known to the Buddha that the masters of various philosophical schools in their country were preaching so many different doctrines that they did not know which to believe and they asked him for advice.

The Buddha replied:

"Believe nothing on the faith of traditions, even though they have been held in honour for many generations and in divers places. Do not believe a thing because many people speak of it. Do not believe on the faith of the sages of the past. Do not believe what you yourself have imagined, persuading yourself that a God inspires you. Believe nothing on the sole authority of your masters or priests. After examination, believe what you yourself have tested and found to be reasonable, and conform your conduct thereto."

Whatever modifications the Mahâyânists subsequently introduced into the teachings of the Buddha, they did not compromise on this point. It might almost be said that they emphasised the necessity for spiritual independence.

The few passages from the ritual of mystic initiations quoted in this book, testify to the importance that the Lamaists attach to it. One may here see quite clearly that the true "initiation" is that which the mind confers upon itself, and that all others are but means of attaining to this.

And so, although the abbots of Gahlden, as successors of Tsong Khapa, enjoyed a certain pre-eminence amongst the *gelugspas*, this pre-eminence always remained purely honorific and they never exercised any effective spiritual authority whatsoever over monks and laymen belonging to this sect. The title of "head" of the "yellow cap" sect – sometimes given to them by foreign writers and also employed by myself as a name akin to those familiar to Westerners – really indicates no official function of any kind.

Nor have the abbots of Gahlden been specially mentioned as masters of mysticism, possessed of some special oral tradition (*dam nag*) concerning methods of psychic training. The monopoly of the *dam nags*, and consequently of the initiations related to them, would appear to be held by the sects of the "red caps" whose roots are buried in the past, at a time when the religious world of Tibet was still in communication with the Buddhists of India.

Several centuries before the birth of Tsong Khapa, two powerful Grand Lamas, he of the Karmapas and more especially he of the Sakyapas, had seized the temporal powers by supplanting the feudal lords who had shared the country since the extinction of the last royal dynasty. Indeed, the Grand Lama of Sakya had become a real king, by the grace of the Emperor Kublaï Khan (the first Chinese emperor of the Mongol dynasty, thirteenth century) who, as suzerain of Tibet, had appointed him to the sovereignty.

Nevertheless, Tsong Khapa's reform, though introducing a stricter discipline in some of the Lama clergy, had by no means quenched within them the thirst after worldly possessions and dignities. The power exercised by the Grand Lama of Sakya excited the jealousy of the abbots of Gahlden.

Lobzang Gyatso, the fifth of them in order of succession,

achieved his ends by obtaining the support of a Mongol prince who had seized Tibet. This prince destroyed the power of the red sects. Large numbers of their monasteries were razed to the ground and others confiscated on behalf of the "yellow caps", their members being forcibly incorporated with these latter. The temporal sovereignty of Tibet was given to Lobzang Gyatso by his Mongol protector, as it had been given about four centuries earlier by another Mongol, Kublaï Khan, to the Grand Lama of Sakya.

After his elevation to royalty, Lobzang Gyatso had proclaimed himself to be an avatar of the Bodhisattva Chenrezigs, the protector of Tibet, and had set forward his own master as an avatar of the mystic Buddha Öpagmed.

The monastery of Gahlden, hidden among the mountains in a deserted region, could no longer afford refuge to the monk who was now king, although he was obliged to retain on the throne a religious character and even to wear monastic garments.

In the seventh century, the great king Srongbsten Gampo had built a fortress-palace, that was now in ruins, on the hill of the Potala at Lhasa. No site could have been found more suitable for the new sovereign. Tradition had consecrated this spot, connecting it with the memory of the most famous of Tibetan kings, and the curious aspect of the hill, rising isolated in the midst of an immense valley, made it eminently fit to serve as the pedestal of the abode of a divine sovereign. Lobzang Gyatso began the construction of the extraordinary edifice which, with its successive additions from time to time, was destined to become the modern Potala.

We are very far from the mysterious sanctuary built up in the imagination of certain people. Assuredly the Potala comprises a monastery of which the Dalai Lama is the abbot, but it is a monastery like all others as regards the rites celebrated in it. The only difference it offers is its distinctly aristocratic character. Only the sons of noble and wealthy families are accepted as monks. The expense incumbent upon these latter is great. They are expected to meet a host of expenses necessitated by the upkeep of the monastery and its guests, thus paying for the honour of being a *trapa*[1] of the Dalai Lama's private monastery. It is fitting to add that the merit of the candidates has also to be considered when they demand admission to this group of the elect. Wealth and noble ancestors are not sufficient; the monks of the Potala are supposed to be learned, and this as a rule they are. These sons of opulent families, who are exempt from all material cares, are provided from childhood with the best teachers, and as they have absolutely nothing else to do than to study, they find no great difficulty in acquiring the kind of scholastic erudition which Tibet holds in honour.

We are still a long distance from the heights of mysticism. The truth is that we must not expect to find them at the Potala any more than in any of the great State monasteries: Sera, Gahlden, Depung, and their annexes close to Lhasa. In these great Lamaic institutions are to be found men of remarkable intelligence, erudite scholars, philosophers slightly sceptical or epicurean, and also a small number of Lamas who are truly pious in the special form of Buddhist piety which takes the form of charity. As for Tibetan mystics, like their Indian brethren, they prefer solitude and choose to live in the desert.

Truth compels us to divest the Potala and its ruling sovereign of the fantastic halo which some have gratuitously woven about them; but we need not pass to the other extreme, and conclude that the Dalai Lama and his learned monks are

---

[1] *Trapa*, "pupil", is the title assumed by all members of the clergy who are not ecclesiastical dignitaries. The latter alone have the right to the title of Lama. Nevertheless, it is the custom, when speaking to learned or aged monks, to give them the courtesy title of Lama.

deprived of a secret doctrine withheld from them by certain almost inaccessible masters.

I think I have on several occasions clearly expressed myself on this point. There is nothing esoteric about Buddhism, either in its Lamaic form or among the more orthodox sects. The Buddha distinctly and definitely stated this to his cousin and disciple Ânanda whom certain men, ignorant of the Buddhist Scriptures, have very inconsiderately designated as having been entrusted with secret teaching.

"I have taught the doctrine without any restriction whatsoever, Ânanda, making no distinction between the exoteric and the esoteric. I am not like those Masters who keep their fists closed or who conceal certain things,"[1] declares the Buddha shortly before his death to his cousin when the latter asks him if he has nothing more to teach his disciples.

It follows that we cannot doubt but that the Dalai Lamas have every facility for receiving full instruction in the noblest philosophical and mystical doctrines of Lamaism. For my part, I am in a position to assert that the Dalai Lama[2] whom I met was profoundly versed in these doctrines and was fully capable of expounding them.

Angkurs are conferred upon the Dalai Lamas as upon any other adept in Lamaism. Tsong Khapa, their great spiritual ancestor, applied for "initiations" from several masters, not only in his youth, but when already famous and at the head of a numerous body of disciples.

Remember that the fact of receiving an *angkur* does not necessarily indicate the complete inferiority of the recipient to him who confers it. There are cases where two Lamas exchange *angkurs* in mutual initiation, or – to remain faithful

---

[1] Mahâparinibbâna sutta.
[2] He was the thirteenth Dalai Lama and died on 17 December 1933.

to the meaning of the word *angkur* – communicate to each other the different powers they respectively possess.

Naturally it is impossible to know what mystic *angkurs* a Dalai Lama has received, or even if he has ever turned to the mystic path. It is equally impossible to know what *angkurs* a Dalai Lama is capable of conferring. That is a secret which each master keeps to himself. What it is possible to ascertain is that the Dalai Lamas have never claimed to be Masters of mysticism, or spiritual guides, and that it is not to the Potala that those in search of spiritual enlightenment apply.

The *angkurs* conferred upon a few privileged individuals by the Dalai Lama are more particularly of the exoteric order; the one most frequently administered is that of Chenrezigs.

Thirteen Dalai Lamas succeeded to the Potala before the coming of the present monk-king. Most of them died young, and only two of them – for very different reasons – became famous.

The first of these is Lobzang Gyatso, frequently called "the Great Fifth". It was he who acquired temporal power; as sovereign he left the reputation of a capable energetic man, not disdaining to display the pomp and ceremony that are so pleasing to the Tibetans.

The celebrity of his successor, the sixth of the Dalai Lamas, has a less honourable origin, though he merits special mention because of a tradition which affects our subject.

The child, whose evil destiny had caused him to be regarded as the reincarnation of Lobzang Gyatso and an avatar of Chenrezigs, would appear to have been remarkably intelligent. Doubtless he would have been both a brilliant king and a gracious poet, if the Dalai Lamas, although autocrats, had not been compelled to observe a monastic discipline which enjoins strict celibacy. This proved to be the undoing of Tsang Yang Gyatso.

The title of avatar (*tulku*) cannot be repudiated; a Dalai Lama does not abdicate. The young man whose ambition could not hold in check the appeal of the senses set reprobation at defiance and gave full rein to his evil propensities.

Tsang Yang Gyatso wrote many poems that are still extremely popular in Tibet. They give expression to the anguish and struggles of the poor Grand Lama. Here is a free translation of a few of them:

As one gazes upon the luscious peach
Hanging from the top of the peach-tree, out of reach,
So I gazed upon the maiden of noble birth
Charming and full of youthful vigour.

Furtively proceeding along the path,
I met my beloved all beauteous and perfumed,
An azure turquoise which I found
And then had to cast aside.

Maiden towards whom my heart leaps,
Could'st thou but be mine,
I should think I had won
The most precious of Ocean's pearls.

Peace, you prattling parrots (those who blamed him),
In the willow wood the *djolmo*[1] wishes to sing
Whether terrible or not
The gods and demons in wait behind me,
I would make mine the sweet apple
Which is here before me.

[1]The name of a singing bird.

I went to the most excellent of Lamas[1]
To beseech him to direct my mind;
And I was unable, even in his presence, to fix it upon
    him,
It escaped and flew away to my love.

In vain do I evoke the face of my master,
It does not image itself in my mind;
But, without my calling it, the face of my beloved
Rises in my mind, with overwhelming effect.

My thoughts travel on and on, bearing me far away,
Were they but to fly thus towards the holy Doctrine,
In this very life, forsooth,
I should become a Buddha.

In the east, on the mountain-top
Shines the moon's white splendour.
The visage of my beloved
Flits to and fro before my mind.

With mind far away,
My nights are sleepless;
The days bring me not the object of my desire
And my heart is very weary.

The following two lines, giving a precise description of
the sixth Dalai Lama, are known to all Tibetans:

---

[1]The text mentions a "lama santal". The name of the precious sandalwood,
used as a qualificative, in Tibetan fashion, indicates a person's excellence or
superiority.

At the Potala I am the noble Tsang Yang Gyatso
But in the town I am a libertine, a rake of note.

What did the Tibetans think of the strange way in which
the august Chenrezigs appeared before them in this strange
avatar? Faith makes one see all things under a special aspect;
notwithstanding the eccentricities of Tsang Yang Gyatso, the
majority of Tibetans continued to believe in him.

But the Chinese, who at the time exercised effective lord-
ship over Tibet, showed less patience. They deposed the
too-ardent Dalai Lama and finally put him to death, to the
great indignation of the Tibetans. In vain did they offer
another young man whom they had elected, alleging that
Tsang Yang Gyatso was not the genuine avatar and had been
appointed by mistake. The faithful refused to acknowledge
him as Dalai Lama and impatiently awaited the reincarnation
of the unfortunate Tsang Yang Gyatso.

On this matter Tsang Yang Gyatso is said to have left the
following prediction. Like the preceding lines, it is very popular in Tibet:

> White bird, lend me thy wings,
> I shall not go far away;
> After going round Litang
> I shall soon return here.

There was actually discovered in the province of Litang
(Eastern Tibet) a child who answered to the conditions neces-
sary for recognition as the reincarnation of the defunct Dalai
Lama.

What has gone before is an account of historical facts.
The reason I have dwelt upon them at length is that I might

make known the strange personality of Tsang Yang Gyatso.

He would seem to have been initiated into certain methods which permit – or perhaps even encourage – what appears to us debauchery, and would indeed be so in the case of any other than an "initiate" into that singular training of which it is difficult to speak outside a medical treatise.

What leads one to suspect that Tsang Yang Gyatso was an adept in these practices is, among other indications, an evidently fantastic story, though one whose symbolism is perfectly clear to anyone acquainted with the training in question. Here is the story:

Tsang Yang Gyatso happened to be on the upper terrace of his palace at the Potala, accompanied by those who were scandalised by his licentious conduct.

"Yes, I have mistresses," he said in answer to their reproaches, "and you who blame me also have them, but do you think that the possession of a woman is the same thing for you as it is for me?"

He then approached the edge of the terrace and made water over the balustrade. The liquid flow descended to the base of the Potala and then "ascended" to the higher terrace and returned into the Grand Lama along the same channel by which it had gone forth.

The Grand Lama now addressed those around him:

"You do the same," he said, "and, if you cannot, understand that my relations with women are different from yours."

Related in this way, the story appears simply burlesque but we may well believe that it is the distorted version of a real happening.

A certain class of Tibetan occultists teach a mode of training that is half physical and half psychic, comprising such strange practices as causing the return into the body of the seminal fluid which is on the point of being expended in sexual union, or reabsorbing it when it has actually been ejected.

Curious reasons are alleged in explanation of the utility of these exercises. In the first case, it is not simply a matter of retaining within oneself the energy which Tibetans regard as being contained in the seed of life – for ascetics who strictly practise celibacy do this naturally – but of exciting this latent energy and then refraining from expending it. In the second case, it is said that the energy inherent in the sperm may be enriched, during coition, with an element of feminine energy which it appropriates to itself and carries away with it when reabsorption takes place.

Some imagine that in this way they can practise a kind of subtle vampirism by engrossing the psychic force of those women marked with special signs, whom they look upon as incarnate fairies.

The distinctive sign of those capable of this strange exploit consists in wearing the hair long, bound in a single plait hanging down the back. Nowadays, however, a considerable number of so-called *naljorpas* have adopted this coiffure "without having the right to do so", an "initiate" informed me.

Novices train themselves in this practice by exercising themselves in drawing up a liquid (water or milk) along the canal of the urethra.

Much might be said about this singular aspect of the secret science of Tibet. We may be sure that, however ridiculous or offensive these practices may appear to us, there is nothing lewd or lustful about those who become addicted to them, nor do they in any way tend to sensual enjoyment.

Hindus are acquainted with the special training just mentioned; we find it described in various works on *hatha yoga*. Have the Tibetans borrowed it from them through the Nepalese with whom they have maintained a constant relationship throughout the centuries that immediately followed the introduction of Buddhism into their land? This is quite possible; nevertheless, the origin of these practices – as indeed that of the whole Tantric system with which they are related – is still a mystery to us.

Both in India and in Tibet there are some who maintain – and not altogether without foundation – that the terms employed in describing these realistic practices are not really connected with the objects they seem to indicate. Indeed, the Tibetans have a mystic language called the "language of the Dakînîs", the words of which, borrowed from the vulgar tongue, have a special meaning for initiates.

And so one may wonder if those who declare the figurative interpretation to be the only genuine one are arbitrarily purging a doctrine which was originally very material, or if, on the other hand, the partisans of grossly material practices have debased a doctrine which was originally spiritual.

Probably no other alternative will offer itself to the mind of a Westerner, but such is not the case with Orientals who do not set up, between the things of the mind and those of the body, the watertight compartment which centuries of education incites us to find therein.

An "initiate" in pursuit of experiences, a mere slave of senses too exacting, or perhaps both at once, the sixth Dalai Lama is very sympathetically remembered. A sort of unofficial and half-secret cult is paid to him by the good folk of Lhasa. In this city a mysterious red sign marks certain houses in which tradition has it that Tsang Yang Gyatso met his fair friends. At times the common people furtively touch these signs with their brow[1] in homage of the young libertine who was an avatar of

---

[1] Tibetans touch with their forehead religious books, statues of the Buddha or other deities, or even the garments worn by Lamas whom they revere. By this gesture they testify to their veneration and at the same time "bless themselves" with the object they touch.

the mystic Lord of Infinite Compassion.

Since Tsang Yang Gyatso offers me the opportunity, I think I will now relate a story I heard, connected with the subject in question.

The hero of this story is the famous Vedantine philosopher Sri Sankarâcharya (the Master Sankara) to whom the Brahmans are indebted for having restored them to their privileged condition which had been greatly compromised by the preaching of the rationalistic and anti-ritualistic doctrine of the Buddha.

The personality of this Master, as it appears to us in biographies that are three parts legendary, must have been an extremely remarkable one. Unfortunately, a sort of caste politics would appear to have obscured the keenness of his intellect, making Sankarâcharya the champion of baneful social theories completely opposed to the lofty pantheism which he preached.

The following story is very well known in India where it has circulated for many centuries without the disciples of the great philosopher being able to realise the ridicule it cast upon their master. Of recent years, and perhaps influenced by Occidental ideas adopted during their education in English colleges, certain Hindu intellectuals have been made aware of the grotesque character of the adventure attributed to Sankarâcharya, and now repudiate it. Nevertheless, some adepts of Hindu Tantrism defend its authenticity and give it a meaning that refers to the kind of training into which Tsang Yang Gyatso appears to have been initiated. I hasten to say that this opinion is held only by a few Tantrikas.

Well, as Sankara was journeying through India in quest of eminent adversaries with whom he might contend in philosophical jousts, as was the custom of the day, he challenged a master named Mandana, a disciple of the celebrated Batta, who taught the ritualistic doctrine of Karma-mimansa, according to which salvation could be obtained only by religious services, sacraments, sacrifices to deities, etc., Sancharâcharya affirmed, on the contrary, that salvation is the fruit of Knowledge.

It was agreed that the one who should be worsted in the discussion should become the disciple of the victor and adopt his mode of living. Consequently, as Mandana was a layman and Sankarâcharya an ascetic (*sannyâsin*), if the arguments of the former triumphed, the latter would have to lay aside his religious garb and take to himself a wife, whereas, in the contrary event, Mandana should be compelled to leave his wife and home and put on the orange cotton robe worn in India by all who have made the great renunciation.[1]

The controversy took place in public. After a prolonged defence, Mandana found himself barren of further arguments and Sankarâcharya was on the point of claiming him as his disciple when the wife of the vanquished layman, a profound scholar named Bharati, intervened:

---

[1] The Hindu *sannyâsin* is dead not only to this world but to all others. He has celebrated his own funeral service and, to indicate that nothing any longer binds him to human society, has burnt the girdle worn by Hindus as the distinctive mark of their caste. On the day of his ordination, he pronounces the formula of the threefold renunciation: *Aum bhu sanyastan mayâ. Aum bhuva sanyastan mayâ. Aum sva sanyastan mayâ* By this he declares that he renounces our world and the two others next to it in the scale of the seven superimposed regions which, according to the Hindus, rise above the earth. This is often explained as the renunciation of the things of this world, that of the world of ancestors, i.e. the after-death life afforded by the persistence of the recollection of our personality in the memory of future generations, and that of the world of the gods, i.e. of all paradises whatsoever.

No Hindu except a *sannyâsin* dare utter this formula which is regarded as sacred and awe-inspiring. He who uttered it would automatically become a *sannyâsin*, as all his family, social and spiritual connections would be irremediably broken off.

"The Holy Scriptures," she said to Sankara, "declare that husband and wife form but one person. By defeating my husband, therefore, you have triumphed over only the half of our being. Your victory can be regarded as complete only if I too am overcome by you."

The philosopher could answer nothing in return, for Bharati's claim was based on orthodox texts. He recommenced a new discussion with her. The lady speedily discovered that her learning and skill in controversy could not vie with those of her opponent and so, with the skill peculiar to women, she saved the situation by a stratagem.

The Sacred Scriptures of the Hindus include sensual love amongst the sciences. Bharati asked her ascetic interlocutor certain questions on this particular subject. He was abashed and bewildered.

Since early youth, he explained to the learned and crafty woman, philosophy had occupied all his thoughts, and as a *sannyâsin* who had taken the vow of celibacy, women and all that concerned them were altogether alien to him. Nevertheless he did not think that his ignorance was irreparable; he believed himself quite capable of acquiring the knowledge he lacked. It was but a matter of time. Would not the learned Bharati grant him a month for self-instruction? At the end of the month, he would resume the discussion.

And now Bharati proved herself to be imprudent. She underestimated the powers of her opponent; or perhaps she thought that so short a time would be insufficient to enable him to master the science required. She therefore acquiesced, and Sankarâcharya went in search of instructors.

About that time, a rajah named Amaruka happened to die. Sankara, who could not begin his studies in the person of the philosopher-ascetic already so well known, regarded this death as an exceptional opportunity which he might utilise.

He ordered his disciples carefully to keep his body in a place apart, then, making use of his power as a *yogin*, his "double" left his body and entered into that of the prince which was being conveyed to the funeral pile. The resurrected Amaruka was led back to his palace to the very great joy of many *ranis*, his lawful spouses, and a considerable number of pretty concubines.

Sankara proved himself a zealous scholar, agreeably surprising his women-folk who had been somewhat neglected by the defunct rajah, who was advancing in age. The ministers and members of the Council also remarked that the intelligence of their prince had become considerably greater since his resurrection. The present sovereign seemed completely different from the obtuse-minded rajah whom they had known for years.

It followed that both the women of the palace and the members of the State Council came to suspect that the spirit of a powerful *siddha*[1] was making use of the body of the dead Amaruka. Fearing lest he might leave them and resume his own body, the ministers ordered that search should be made throughout the country for an inanimate body hidden in some remote spot, and that as soon as it were found, it should be burned.

Sankara had become so profoundly absorbed in his studies that he had lost all memory of his real personality and had not the slightest thought of re-entering the body of the philosopher-ascetic which was lying somewhere under the guardianship of a few disciples.

Nevertheless, when the day appointed for his return had elapsed, finding that their master did not come back, they began to be uneasy. Coming to have knowledge of the search

[1]A man possessed of super-normal powers.

that had been ordered, their uneasiness became blank dismay. A few of them hastily departed for the palace of Amaruka, succeeded in entering therein and, beneath the rajah's windows, sang a philosophical hymn composed by Sankarâcharya himself.

This song stirred the memory of their master. His "double" instantly left the body of Amaruka and returned into his own which had just been discovered and was already actually on the funeral pile. . . .

Now fully competent, our philosopher returned to Bharati, amazed her by his wide learning and the lady had to admit defeat.

The real facts have been distorted, say those who in this story are determined to see things never intended. The truth is that Sankara, at some moment of his career, must have acquired a psychic force which he lacked, by means of practices requiring intercourse with woman. I leave the responsibility for this opinion to those who profess it.

However it may have been with the great Hindu philosopher, it appears certain that Milarespa, a very chaste and stern bachelor, ordered his disciple Restchungpa to cohabit for some time with a woman whom he pointed out to him, and tradition has it that the couple chose to dwell in a lonely mountain cave, a detail calculated to show that the adepts of these practices are not libertines and have other things in view than sense gratification.[1]

Indeed, whatever might be the object in view, Buddhism recognises no practice of this kind, and in Tibet it has no place in official Lamaism.

---

[1]Another tradition says that it was not Restchungpa who needed a companion. Rather was it the woman, herself a disciple of Milarespa, who was to derive special benefit from the company of Restchungpa. Of course, the couple separated, and the temporary husband and wife lived as anchorites.

The rôle of the Tashi Lamas is identical with that of the Dalai Lamas. The only difference between them is that the latter, while avatars, are temporal rulers of Tibet. The practical results of this difference are considerable. This was ascertained when the late Tashi Lama[1] was compelled to flee from Tibet to escape from his powerful colleague.

As the Tashi Lamas do not officially concern themselves with politics and live in retirement in their holdings in the province of Tsang, they are regarded by some as more exclusively religious than the Dalai Lamas, though, in this respect, the main body of the Tibetans make no distinction between them.

No more than the Dalai Lamas are the Tashi Lamas looked upon as the representatives of lines of Masters handing down to one another a traditional oral teaching. Their official title is *Tsang Penchen rimpoche*. *Penchen* is the Tibetan adaptation of the Sanskrit word *pandita*, meaning a scholar, more especially one versed in philosophy. This title, then, attributes to the Tashi Lamas the character of a learned philosopher rather than that of a contemplative mystic.

The Tsang Penchens are the Grand Lamas of the monastery of Tashilhumpo (heap of prosperity) at Shigaze. From there they received the name of Tashi Lama by which foreigners call them. This name is not current in Tibet.

Whatever may be thought of the popular theory which looks upon these Lamas as successive reincarnations of one and the same individual, it seems evident that all the Tashi Lamas are noted for pleasant dispositions and extreme benevolence. This face has been ascertained by travellers who have visited them in past centuries, while the welcome I myself

---

[1] He died in November 1937 on the borders of Tibet when he was returning home after ten years of sojourn in China. His successor is a young man; a few years younger than the Dalai Lama.

received from the late Tashi Lama enables me to add my own testimony.

Coming immediately after the Dalai Lamas and the Tashi Lamas is another great avatar, that of Dorje Phagmo,[1] who manifests as a woman and whose *tulku* is the Lady Lama abbess of a monastery situated near Lake Yamdok in Southern Tibet. This lofty personality of the Lamaic world is no more supposed to be particularly learned in mysticism than are the two eminent *tulkus* of Chenrezigs and Öpagmed – the Dalai and Tashi Lamas.

In reality, no Tibetan expects to see these Avatar Grand Lamas become heads of philosophical schools, lead disciples along the path of wisdom, or confer mystic initiations. Emanations of beings superior to the gods, they are essentially protectors.[2] Their presence in Tibet, the Tibetans themselves believe, ensures widespread prosperity and happiness, and the blessings they solicit from the kindness of these exalted Lamas are such as find expression in material advantages either in this life or in another.

---

[1] A female deity of the Tantric pantheon.

[2] Kyabgön rimpoche (skyabs mgon rinpoche), "precious protector", is the title by which the Dalai Lama is known to his subjects. The title Dalai Lama is used only by foreigners. The Tashi Lama (it is a Mongolian word which signifies "Ocean Lama") also has the right to the title of "precious protector" but it is not so frequently given to him except at Shigaze. The disciples of a few Grand Lamas, living far from the centre of Tibet, sometimes call them "protector"; such flattery could not be attempted either at Lhasa or at Shigaze. A heavy fine would be the least punishment that would be inflicted on those who indulged in it or on the Lama who authorised it. See pp. 240-44 for a note on the present position of the Dalai Lama and the Penchen Lama since the establishment of the Communist régime in China and the re-establishment of Chinese suzerainty over Tibet.

6

THE LESSER AND THE
GREATER VEHICLE

Hînayâna and Mahâyâna are familiar terms to those
who have read works on Buddhism; it would therefore appear superfluous to explain them. Nevertheless, as the meaning given to them by the Buddhists, especially by the initiate Lamaists, diverges widely from that
current in the West, it is fitting to deal with it at this stage.

In the language of the Orientalists, the expressions
Hînayâna (in Tibetan, *theg men*) and mahâyâna (in Tibetan,
thegpa chenpo), apply to a division of Buddhism into the primitive doctrine and more recent doctrines, presenting either
developments or a corruption of the ancient teaching.

It is not my purpose to expound the philosophical conceptions that characterise the two "vehicles". Moreover, this
division of the Buddhist world into two clearly distinct factions
is wholly theoretical and but slightly conformable with the
facts of the case.

In the first place, the name Hînayâna, "lower vehicle",
formerly given by the orthodox to their opponents, is not
accepted by them. The Sinhalese, the Burmese, the Siamese,
and all the Buddhists whom foreigners include among the
Hînayâists, do not consider themselves – and quite rightly – as

inferior to their co-religionists in China, Japan, and Tibet in matters touching Buddhist philosophy. On the contrary, they declare that they are in possession of the only authentic doctrine, that of the Theras: the Ancients.

The Buddhists in the lands of Northern Asia, whom foreigners call Mahâyânists without distinction, are more discreet, as a rule, in accepting the title.

Here I will deal only with the Tibetans, more particularly with the masters of mysticism who teach a *dam nag* and confer esoteric and mystic initiations.

It has been said that the expression "great vehicle" indicates a doctrine more acceptable to the majority than that of the Ancients and which is more capable of bearing multitudes of the faithful to salvation.

This interpretation – which indeed I have not found to be current in Asia – is unknown to the Lamaists. In their opinion, the mahâyâna must be understood as a "great" vehicle, in the sense of being superior, lofty.

If they are told that the elaboration of the Mahâyâna doctrines must be attributed to Asvagosha, to Nâgârjuna or some other Buddhist philosopher, they strongly protest against this opinion. Their reply is that these masters taught doctrines belonging to the "great vehicle" but they did not invent it. This "great vehicle" has existed from all time; it consists of various lofty teachings which vulgar minds cannot understand. It follows that, according to the Lamaists, instead of being a spacious vehicle, easy of access to the masses, the Mahâyâna is rather a very distant vehicle accessible only to the êlite.

The Lamaist mystics do not regard the whole of their canonical Scriptures as belonging entirely to the Mahâyâna. They include in the lower vehicle works dealing with precepts of ordinary morality, the rules of monastic discipline and everything in any way connected therewith.

Salvation, they never cease repeating, is a purely spiritual matter; it is the possession of "knowledge", the liberation (*tharpa* or *tolwa*)[1] from delusion, and all these precepts and rules contribute thereto only as a preparatory training which refines the mind.

The Lamaists do not acknowledge two "vehicles" only. They speak of many "vehicles" each of the philosophical systems that we include in the Mahâyâna attempting to assert its own importance.

All the same, the "vehicles" usually mentioned may be reduced to the following:

1. The lower vehicle (*theg men*).
2. The vehicle of the *rang sangyais*, i.e. "of the Buddhas by and for themselves", who do not preach the Doctrine.
3. The vehicle of the *Changchub semspas*, who devote all their energy to the practice of boundless compassion and work for the welfare and enlightenment of mankind.
4. The supremely excellent vehicle (*blana med pa thegpa*).

The lower vehicle, more frequently called the vehicle of the "hearers" (*nien thös kyi thegpa*), corresponds to the Hînayâna. It leads to Nirvâna, by a very long route, the minds incapable of apprehending the subtle doctrines of the Mahâyâna. Besides, say the Tibetans, its adepts aim only at freeing themselves personally from sorrow and grief without working for the salvation of others, and for this reason they are spiritually inferior to the altruistic bodhisattvas (*Changchub semspa*).

The judgement thus delivered by the Tibetans upon the "hearers" is erroneous and proceeds from a complete lack of

[1]Written *grolwa*.

understanding not only of the original Buddhist doctrine but also of its philosophical and mystical developments in the Mahâyâna, as we shall subsequently discover.

The vehicle of the *rang sangyais*, as conceived by the Lamaists, is that of pure intellectuality. The *rang sangyais* is an authentic Buddha. He has acquired knowledge by investigation, introspection and contemplation, and he now enjoys the fruit of his spiritual enlightenment. He does not preach the doctrine nor do any work that aims at the good of others. The portrait given of him by Lamaists sets him forth as a super-intellectual, enclosed in an ivory tower. The name sometimes given to him is "he who comprehends only one cause", meaning that he understands the "Void" but not compassion.

This personage is unpopular in Tibet. There they charge him with being egoistical, without seeming to perceive that he strongly resembles the hero so extolled in the "supremely excellent doctrine" (*blana med pa*) who raises himself to the state of absolute non-activity.

The vehicle of the *Changchub semspas* (Sanskrit: *bodhisattva*) is the "great vehicle", the Mahâyâna strictly so-called. He is characterised by the object of his adepts, which is not Nirvâna but the state of the bodhisattva whose heart overflows with compassion for the sufferings and sorrows of others and who has power to succour them. At all events, that is his most striking feature. In Tibet, however, this compassion, if it is to be acknowledged as Mahâyânic, must be accompanied by comprehension of the "Void".

Lack of this comprehension would reduce compassion to the lower level of ordinary pity.

Tong gnid nyingdje zung jug,[1] "Void and Compassion combined", is the motto of the Tibetan adepts of the great

[1]Written *stong ñid sñing rdje zung hjug*.

vehicle. The bodhisattva practically exercises his compassion when he has freed himself from the illusion which creates belief in the reality of the world as we perceive it. His mental attitude, difficult to understand by those who have not attained to it themselves, is clearly described in the work entitled *The Diamond Cutter*. There we read that "it is when the bodhisattva no longer believes in anything that the time has come for him to offer gifts", and that only then are these gifts effective. It is also said that "when the bodhisattva has brought to the state of Nirvâna a greater number of beings than the grains of sand on the banks of the Ganges, he must understand that he has saved no one." Why is this? – Because if he believes he has saved any number of beings, he still retains the idea of the "self", and in that case he would not be a bodhisattva.

These are abstruse doctrines the very terms of which can with difficulty be translated into Occidental tongues, while at the same time they require long commentaries.

The fourth vehicle is the *blana med pa thegpa*, literally, "there is none superior".

Its adepts profess, amongst other doctrines, that Nirvâna and the world of phenomena (*nangsi*)[1] are fundamentally identical, two aspects of one and the same thing, or rather, two modes, equally illusive, of envisaging Reality.

Apart from these four vehicles there are also the mystic vehicle (*snags kyi thegpa*), the Tantric or magic vehicle (*rgyud kyi thegpa*), and certain others.

The rôle and personality of the bodhisattva are differently understood in these many vehicles, but all assign him an important place and it is usual to receive the *angkur* of the bodhisattvas before finding oneself admitted to the mystic "initiations".

[1]Written *snang srid*.

It may be doubted whether the Buddha himself made the bodhisattvas the subject of his preaching. The stories of his past lives – the Jatakas – in which he appears as bodhisattva, are manifestly the invention of an inferior order of devotees who have remodelled Hindu stories or invented others of the same kind. Besides, the conduct of the historical Buddha was exempt from the eccentricities which distinguish many bodhisattvas. Nor does his teaching encourage them. The model he sets before the disciple is the calm figure of the *arahan*, the sage who has completely cast off the ten fetters,[1] who has attained immovable serenity of mind and who lives in Nirvâna.

Subsequently, those among the Buddhists whose mind could not rise to the height of this type of spiritual perfection, contrasted the bodhisattva with the arahan. They made of him a fantastic hero whose inordinate charity often expressed itself in unlikely actions, though occasionally in deeds offensive to common sense or even frankly cruel or immoral.

The most popular bodhisattva story, the one that draws tears from thousands of simple believers from the farthest extremity of tropical Ceylon to the northern steppes of Mongola, is that of Vessantara.

Vessantara has made a vow never to refuse to give what is asked of him, in order that by this accumulation of sacrifices and good deeds he may make himself fit to become a Buddha.

[1]The ten fetters which prevent one from attaining final liberation are: (1) belief in "self"; (2) doubt; (3) faith in the efficacy of rites and ceremonies; (4) sensual desires; (5) anger; (6) The desire to live in a world less material than ours (the world of "pure form"); (7) the desire to live in a still subtler world (the "formless" world); (8) pride; (9) restlessness; (10) ignorance.

(6) and (7) may be interpreted as that attachment to existence which inclines the one who experiences it – if he disdains the kind of existence passed by those inhabiting the present material world – to desire life in the higher forms of existence, and yet to continue living a personal life. This desire is bound up with belief in "self".

Being a prince and heir to the throne, it comes about that he gives an enemy the magic jewel which secures prosperity and victory over his father's kingdom.[1] Possessed of this talisman, the enemy invades the land and massacres its inhabitants. Our hero's serenity is in no way disturbed by this disaster. He has remained faithful to his vow – that alone was of any importance.

His father's ministers show scant appreciation of transcendal virtue of this kind; they exile him. His faithful wife insists on sharing his lot, with their two children. And so they come to be living in the forest, in a miserable little hut. An old brahman appears. He has no one to serve him, and so he asks that Vessantara's children shall be his slaves. Immediately and gladly he gives them to the brahman. The little girl and her brother beg their father to keep them, as the wicked brahman treats them brutally, but the prince will not retract his vow. He even congratulates himself on having had so fine an opportunity of manifesting the excellence of his charity. Soon another opportunity is afforded him: this time he gives his wife. Finally he submits to having his eyes torn out, to give them to a blind man so that "he might make use of them to replace his own and recover his sight".

The writers of these tales had a totally different conception from our own of the rights of the head of a family. To them, the latter was the lawful owner of his wife and children. In giving them, he simply disposed of what belonged to him. Consequently the act of the bodhisattva does not offend them; they regard it merely as the renunciation of things very dear to one – hence the greatness of the sacrifice. These barbarous notions being now considerably modified, even in nations still wedded to backward civilisations, the admirers of Vessantara

---

[1]In another version, the jewel is replaced by a white elephant.

frequently assert that his wife and children *consented* to the sacrifice.

Of course the story ends well; the old brahman was a god in disguise who wished to test Vessantara. He gives back to him his children and his wife, another god "restores his eyes that are now more beautiful than ever[1]", the hostile king makes restitution of the jewel. One is tempted to wonder if the conscience of the writers of this story did not make an involuntary protest, and forbid them to allow the victims of their too charitable hero to suffer. Nevertheless, I think it would be a mistake to indulge this opinion. It is the prince alone who interests them, he alone whom they did not wish to abandon in his misfortune; the rest were merely figureheads or supernumeraries of no interest whatsoever.

And so it frequently happens, not only in tales but also in real life, that the extravagant charity which the bodhisattva regards as a duty becomes transformed into nothing less than monstrous egoism.

Some mystic Lamas refuse to recognise this story, celebrated though it be throughout the land, as worthy of being connected with the Mahâyâna. It has all the characteristics of the "lesser vehicle", they told me. Its hero *wishes himself* to enjoy the elation of spreading happiness and enlightenment in the world; he would not rejoice so much if the same happiness and enlightenment were bestowed on mankind by *another* Buddha. He is full of faith in the reality of the "self". It also regards the Buddha as a "person". He has not perceived his real character as being that of universal "wisdom".

---

[1]Another story repeats the same miracle. Prince Kulana has had his eyes torn out by order of the queen, his treacherous mother-in-law, whose lover he refuses to become. His virtue is finally recompensed and his eyes are restored to him.

On the other hand, there are stories of bodhisattvas that have been accepted by these Lamas as representing the Mahâyânist spirit.

The following is one that is very well known throughout Buddhist countries.

A young prince (said to be the historic Buddha in one of his former existences) is wandering through a forest. An abnormal drought has dried up the springs, the beds of the streams are nothing more than sand and pebbles, the leaves of the trees are reduced to dust by the burning heat of the sun, the animals have all fled into other regions. Amid all this desolation, the prince sees, in a thicket close by, a tigress lean and dying, her young all around her. The wild beast sees him also. In her eyes may be read the ardent desire to fling herself upon so near a prey and so give nourishment to her whelps whom she can no longer suckle and who will soon die of hunger like herself. But she lacks the strength to stand on her feet and make the leap. There she remains outstretched, a pitiable object in her maternal distress and her longing for life.

Thereupon the young prince in tender pity turns from the path, and advancing towards the tigress who cannot attack him, offers to her his own body as food.

The finest part of this story is that it scorns the usual miracle at the end. No god intervenes, the prince is devoured alive and the curtain falls upon the mystery of what may follow.

In all probability this is a mere legend, and yet I think – not altogether without reason – that an action of this kind really might take place. It is difficult to fathom the depths of charity and self-abnegation that are attained by certain Buddhist mystics.

The one essentially Mahâyânist act which inspires the veneration of the Lamaist masses for the mythical bodhisattvas like Chenrezigs is their renunciation of Nirvâna.

True, having by dint of virtue won the right to Nirvâna, their intense altruism makes them renounce it in order to continue to help their fellow-mortals – which the Buddhas who have entered Nirvâna can no longer do.

The success of this sentimental lucubration has been enormous in Tibet. We find an echo of it in the numerous rites during which the holy Lamas and other heroes are entreated not to enter Nirvâna in order to continue to protect their fellow-beings.

Nothing could be imagined more opposed to the teaching of Buddhism than the idea that Nirvâna can be rejected.

It is possible to renounce entrance into a paradise which is a definite place, but Nirvâna is essentially the state produced automatically by the extinction of ignorance, and he who has attained to *knowledge* cannot, however much he may wish it, help knowing what he knows.

The masters of mysticism are under no misapprehension on this point, and, notwithstanding their popularity, these erroneous notions regarding the conduct of the bodhisattva find no place in the teachings given to the disciples whom they have admitted into the initiations of the higher degrees.

The desire to become *oneself* a Buddha appears to them to denote a complete misunderstanding of what they call "the mind of Buddha". The human Buddhas – or those who are able to appear under different forms in other worlds – are only manifestations (*tulkus*) of this "mind", which, however, we must guard against conceiving as a "person".

To express their opinion concerning the efforts of legendary bodhisattvas and of those who would like to imitate them, certain Lamas employ strange parables.

Imagine, one of them said to me, that whilst the sun is shining, a man is obstinately determined to light a lamp, *his* lamp, in order to provide light for himself or for someone else. In vain it is pointed out to him that it is broad daylight, that the sun is shedding its radiance upon all things. He refuses to benefit by this radiance, what he desires is a light produced *by himself*. Very likely this man's folly is due to the fact that he does not discern the sunlight; for him it does not exist, an opaque screen prevents him from perceiving it. This screen consists of infatuation of self, of his personality and his works; reasoning (*rtogpas*) as distinct from comprehension (*rtogspa*).

Here we have the whole of Tibetan mysticism, its great principle is: there is nothing to "do", there is to "undo". I have said in another place that the contemplatives amongst the Lamas compared spiritual training to a clearing or weeding process.

Whereas a small élite of thinkers profess these and similar ideas, popular beliefs regarding bodhisattvas flounder more and more in the bog of absurdity and give rise to many a comic incident.

They now provide certain Lamas with the means of justifying discrepancies of conduct calculated to offend the faithful, and of transforming them into praiseworthy deeds of abnegation and devotion. We shall see how this comes about.

The Lama – head of a sect or a line of masters, or simply the abbot of a monastery, but in any event a *tulku*[1] – cleverly spreads abroad the rumour that, after having filled the same abbatial or other seat during his successive reincarnations, he has now reached the last of them. His spiritual perfection has attained the final stage; after his death, he will enter Nirvâna.

The holy Lama or great magician whom he now incarnates ceasing to be reborn in this world, what will be the lot of

[1] The Lamas whom foreigners incorrectly call living Buddhas. See *With Mystics and Magicians in Tibet.*

the faithful whom he has been protecting for centuries past? What will become of these orphans now forsaken and delivered over to innumerable kinds of evil spirits whom the very beneficent and potent Lama was able to keep at a distance? Flocks will now be decimated by disease, hailstorms will ruin the crops, and great numbers of the dead will be unable to attain to the Paradise of the Great Beatitude, whereas by performing the required rites the Lama made its approach so easy for the departed whose families could generously recompense his services.

The Grand Lama cannot envisage all these calamities without his heart bleeding. To prevent his benefactors, laymen and monks, from suffering by his happy release, he will sacrifice himself. He will renounce Nirvâna and continue to reincarnate. But how are the effects of his lofty perfection to be prevented from following their course and removing him from this world? There is only one – a very painful – means: to lapse from virtue, resignedly to commit a sin.

Frequently the sin chosen consists in taking a wife, officially or otherwise, when the Lama is vowed to a state of celibacy.

The marriage of the Grand Lama of the Karmapas, all of whose predecessors from the twelfth century were bachelors, is attributed to a manifestation of charity.

I may add that the Tibetans, born wags for the most part notwithstanding their rustic appearance and their superstitions, generally accept these too compassionate Lamas in a spirit of mocking banter.

I happened, unwittingly, to play a part in one of these comedies, though I must be excused if I do not mention the hero, a kind and very intelligent man, a friend of progress and acquainted with certain Europeans living on the Chinese frontier. As it is possible that they may read these lines and translate them to him, I regard discretion as indispensable.[1]

At that time, I was living in the monastery of Kum Bum. One day I was informed that a lady from Lhasa was journeying in those parts and wished to see me. I welcomed her heartily. In the course of conversation, I learnt that she was the "morganatic" wife of a *tulku*, the abbot of a rich monastery of the sect of the "yellow caps" whose compassion had led him to choose marriage as a means of renouncing Nirvâna. The story amused me. The lady was sumptuously dressed and quite charming. There was even a particular expression in her face that drew my attention.

When she had gone, I said to my servant who had introduced her:

'There is something strange about that woman. She is a *lhamo* (goddess) who has assumed human form.'

I made the remark jestingly and was amazed to find that it was received with the utmost seriousness.

The man to whom I had spoken was a native of Lhasa, and well acquainted with the husband of my pretty visitor, having been his factotum for many years. Anxiously he questioned me:

"Is it quite true, reverend lady, that you noticed particular signs in her?"

"Certainly," I answered, continuing the jest; "she is an incarnated *lhamo*. Her face is of a bluish tint."

The skin of certain Tibetan women of the bronzed type sometimes has a slightly bluish or mauve cast.[2] This fact is supposed to indicate that the one who offers this peculiarity is a fairy incarnate.

---

[1]As, since the above was written, he has died (some ten years ago) I can now mention his name – he was the Lama of the Lob monastery.

[2]We must not imagine that all Tibetan women are dark-complexioned. Many women from the central provinces are very fair and differ from Chinese women in having pink cheeks.

"Then the Lama was right in what he saw at Lhasa," said the servant.

At my request he told me the story of his former master.

The latter happened to be in a house of his at Lhasa. One day, when walking to and fro on the roof-terrace of his house[1] he noticed a young woman sewing on a neighbouring roof.

The Lama, a sturdy man of about thirty, without anything to do in the holy city, was perhaps passing through one of those moments of dull loneliness when he could not help dreaming of the unknown fairy.

Both on the morrow and on the following day he saw her again at the same spot. Without further ado, he sent his factotum – who told me the story – to the parents of the girl to demand her hand in marriage. He justified his request by explaining that, as the result of his super-normal clairvoyance, he had discovered signs which showed her to be a fairy incarnate. In addition, he had understood during his profound meditations that he must marry her so that he might escape from Nirvâna and so benefit the entire neighbourhood.

Such declarations, coming from a Grand Lama and backed up by substantial gifts, could not fail to convince the humble folk whose daughter in this world the "fairy" was. They immediately gave their consent.

Thus it came about that my words proved a valuable confirmation of the Lama's claim. I had noticed on the face of his wife the famous "signs" which hitherto he had probably been the only one to perceive. I could not take back my words . . . the lady was an exiled goddess.

The opinion to which I had given expression was not long in reaching her ears, and finally became known to the

[1]The houses in Tibet have flat roofs; the fine climate of the country makes it possible to use them continually for work or to meet together for conversation.

Lama himself, who was manifestly delighted, as I quickly discovered from the value of the present he sent me in exchange for a few trifles I had given his wife.

Two years afterwards I was his guest amid the grassy solitudes of Northern Tibet where, on the slopes surrounding a deserted valley, stood his monastery, filled with artistic treasures which had been accumulated for centuries past.

Close by, the heroine of this adventure lived in a summerhouse surrounded with gardens. Whether fairy or not, the monastic rule forbade her dwelling within the precincts of the monastery itself.

She showed me her jewels, her garments of precious brocade and cloth of gold . . . a precarious prosperity which might at any moment be brought to an end by the death of her husband or the termination of his caprice for her.

Committing the sin which deprived him of Nirvâna had sufficed to secure the reincarnation of the Grand Lama for the good of his faithful followers. The repetition of this sin was superfluous, and the Lama's ally in his charitable work became useless. The monks, who had not dared to protest against the will of their lord-abbot, would gladly have welcomed the dismissal of the young wife whose presence in their immediate vicinity was an infraction of the discipline of their sect.

The imposing mass of the large monastery with its temples, its venerable palaces, its hermitages proudly built upon the neighbouring peaks, completely eclipsed the poor cottage hiding within its shadow. Poor little fairy![1]

Though the Tibetans discreetly ridicule the Lama who employs marriage as a means of evading Nirvâna, they nevertheless show considerable indulgence in their judgement of his conduct. This indulgence is partly due to the fact that Tibetan

[1]She died a few years after my visit.

morals do not dramatise love. Perhaps because they obey, even unconsciously, the influence of religious doctrines which give to the mind a degree of importance beyond all others, the Tibetans regard the manifestations of sensual passion as both trivial and of slight interest.

Nevertheless, the indulgence shown to the Lama *tulkus* who in one way or another infringe the monastic rules, also springs from the vague fear they inspire almost always, even in the least superstitious of the Tibetans. They are supposed to possess supernormal and magical powers which enable them to discover what is being said about them and to take revenge accordingly. They also believe that the man who blames the Lama who is his protector breaks the psychic bonds which connect them and so automatically deprives himself of his protection.

It may also be added that the masses do not altogether expect that these Grand Lamas should be saints and live an ascetic life. That is a matter exacted only of certain anchorites. The eminent status accorded to the Lama *tulkus*, as I have already stated, is based on the belief that they possess the power effectively to protect their followers, or, in the case of the Dalai Lama, the Tashi Lama and a few other eminent personalities, to protect the whole of Tibet, men, animals, and everything. What is therefore wanted of them is that they should exercise this protective rôle to the best of their ability; means and methods are left to their discretion, as the mass of the people do not regard themselves as capable of fathoming their thoughts.

7

THE TRUE INITIATION

What has previously been said regarding Lamaic "initiations" and the exercises relating thereto, may make one imagine that the word "initiate", in the meaning given to it in other countries and by Western authors, cannot apply to each of the many Tibetans who have received one or other of the various ritual *angkurs* conferred in their country.

I should like to mention once more[1] that the *angkur* in itself is not intended to communicate knowledge, but rather to transmit the power to do some physical or mental act. In the mystic *angkurs*, this power may be interpreted as that of intelligently putting into practice the exercises suitable for developing the faculties requisite to attain spiritual enlightenment. This latter, which the Tibetans express by the terms *tharwar gyourwa* – to become free – is the fruit, not of a rite, but of a mystic experience which cannot be transmitted.

In the biography of Milarespa we find the proof that this interpretation has been that of the Lamas for centuries past.

[1] I am again repeating myself, for we are now considering the most characteristic aspect of the Lamaic "initiations".

I quote this work in preference to so many others capable of supplying the same proof, because it has been translated into English and into French, and so my readers will be able to consult it.

Marpa, the very ritualistic Tantric Lama, and *guru* of Milarespa, neglects neither *angkurs* nor esoteric instruction. Nevertheless, after each ceremony, he never fails to send back his disciples to their cave or hut, there to meditate in solitude.

Then, when he calls them back to give him the results of their meditations, it is solely on these results that he relies to discover whether they have succeeded in "knowing", whether they have "initiated themselves".

However heterodox they may be in many other respects, the Lamaists have kept alive some of the essential principles of Buddhism, especially the one we find in the following words of the Buddha: "Be your own guide and your own torch", a faithful echo of which we find in Tibet: "Men seek protectors and guides outside of themselves and so plunge into grief and pain."[1]

Among the contemplative ascetics of Tibet, these principles would seem to have retained even greater influence than among their co-religionists of the Southern lands. For instance, whereas the latter assert that, lacking the presence of a Buddha on earth at the present time, no one can attain unto the state of an *arhan*, who is fully enlightened and enters alive into Nirvâna, the Lamaist mystics believe that the material presence of a preaching Buddha is by no means indispensable to the obtaining of "Knowledge".

In their opinion, the Doctrine exists, and even apart from the books in which it is set down in writing and the Lamas who teach it, the man who is ready may discover it by meditation

[1]Liturgical text of the rite of "Suppression".

and repeat in himself the spiritual experiences of the Buddha.

In a word, it is here that we have the real "initiation" as conceived by the Masters of mysticism in Tibet. Rightly or wrongly, however, they keep jealousy to themselves their own ideas on the matter. This conception of initiation is one of the profoundest secrets of their esoteric teachings.

And yet, as a Lama wittily said to me: "Esotericism comes into existence only when understanding fails; it is another name for ignorance. A penetrating and investigating mind discovers all things."

Without being gifted with exceptional perspicacity, it is easy to understand the lessons given in numerous histories on the subject of auto-initiation. I will quote one out of many, the details of which – even apart from the matter in hand – do not lack interest as a picture of Tibetan customs.

I did not know Tashi Dadul, but I have every reason to regard his story as perfectly authentic, for it bears the stamp of Tibetan mentality and those who related it to me were quite trustworthy. Nevertheless, even though certain details may have been distorted, it will be valuable in supplying us with information as to the way in which the Tibetans look upon "initiation".

Tashi Dadul was a Gyarong-pa;[1] he belonged to those middle classes of the Tibetan lay population whose members, with few exceptions, engage in commerce. Young and handsome, married to a loving wife of good family, father of a boy of three and head of a prosperous business, Dadul, as the saying goes, had everything necessary to make him happy. And, indeed, he was quite happy until one day he discovered on his strong body the first signs of leprosy.

---

[1] The name given to the members of the Tibetan tribes established in the Chinese valleys on the frontier of Szechuan.

No one in his family, nor in that of his wife, had ever been attacked by this awful malady. He waited, anxiously observing the fatal signs, but soon it was impossible for him to doubt any longer. He consulted the doctors in the neighbourhood, then those of other districts whose reputation and skill had come to his ears, and finally he undertook a long journey to seek help from the doctor of a missionary hospital on the confines of China. The white physician, he thought, would perhaps know of remedies unknown to the Tibetans and the Chinese.

The white man, however, declared himself to be as helpless as his Asiatic colleagues.

Had he examined the patient? Naturally he who told me the story did not know, but I remembered a tragic case of the same kind, a man still young who had come to see me at the monastery of Kum Bum.

He, too, had gone to the white man's hospital in China, but tactlessly he had begun by asking: "Have you anything that will cure leprosy?" He had been answered by a curt negative. Crowds of patients were in the consulting-room, and so he had left without insisting further. I recommended him to return and get himself examined by the doctor, without saying that he thought he was attacked by leprosy. Perhaps the symptoms he had set forth were those of another and a curable disease.

I am relating this personal incident to prevent any idea of the miraculous being associated with the story of Dadul. Any miraculous element it contains is of an exclusively spiritual nature.

Losing all hope in science, Tashi Dadul, like many another desperate individual, turned to religion. In contradistinction to others, however, he did not expect anything in the nature of a prodigy; considering himself to be incurable, he thought only of preparing for death. He also wanted to disappear, not to give to his household – especially his young wife – the spectacle of the hideous creature he was soon to become.

Betaking himself to an anchorite, he asked for his benediction and some method of meditation. The hermit kept him by his side for some time, then he advised him to contemplate Jigsjyed (the Terrible One), the Grand *Yidam* of the sect of the "yellow caps".

Living immured in solitude, he was to adopt no other devotional practice; that one would suffice.

Then the Lama conferred on the patient the *angkur* of Jigsjyed, partially explained to him the symbol of the form and attitude of the *Yidam* and dismissed him.

Speedily Dadul settled his affairs with the living whom he was soon to leave for the tomb. He gave his goods to a relative, entrusted to him his son and the task of supplying the needs of his wife so long as she remained a widow. In addition, he released her from any obligation towards himself; she might marry again if she wished.

The story does not dwell upon the feelings of the unhappy man on thus withdrawing from the world in the full vigour of manhood. The Tibetans are not lavish of detail as to one's deepest emotions. The sentimental outpourings of Milarespa are exceptional in his bleak country . . . but then, Jetsun Milarespa was a poet.

At a distance of several days' march from his village, Dadul built himself a home by erecting a stone wall in front of a fairly large cavern. He had chosen a spot by a hillside, near a stream flowing down into the valley. It was not very difficult to divert a portion of the stream and cause it to flow close by his hut. He stopped up with earth the interstices between the stones which made up his wall. Over the latter, he stretched inside the dwelling a yak's hair covering, like the material with which nomad shepherds make tents. He also built a second outer wall behind which those who came two or three times a year to supply him with food would deposit their sacks of provisions and fuel, without seeing him. Then, still aided by those who had accompanied him, he piled into the cavern the provisions they had brought, coverings, carpets, cushions, and articles of clothing.[1]

Dadul had not gone to the desert to practise austerities, but simply to die there; consequently he had no reason whatsoever to deprive himself, during his last few days, of such comfort as his fortune could procure for him.

When all was over, his friends left him. From the threshold of his future tomb he watched them depart, he heard the tinkling of the bells fastened to the horses' necks gradually fade away. Then the riders disappeared and all was silence. He was alone with death lurking within himself.

He prostrated himself in the direction in which lived the Lama who had initiated him into the rite of Jigsjyed, then, entering his cavern, he again prostrated himself before a *thangka* (a frameless picture on a roll) representing the frightful deity and seated himself on the couch where his body, consumed by leprosy, would one day lie dead, mere food for insects and worms. . . .

Days and weeks passed. At the end of the fourth month, two men brought him some provisions. He heard them unload their animals and place their bags in the "antechamber" of his dwelling. They were invisible, though so close to him.

Had he any desire to speak to them, to know what had become of those so dear to him: his wife and child . . . to ask them if anyone thought of him if his name was ever uttered in his own household? The story does not answer these questions.

[1]This hermitage was in imitation of those used by recluses practising complete isolation. See the description of their dwellings in *With Mystics and Magicians in Tibet*.

It is the custom in Tibet that those who bring food – or anything else – to immured hermits, should not speak to them. The men saw a little smoke rise above the wall that enclosed the "room" of the recluse; he was therefore alive and so they left without a word.

Years passed – fifteen, twenty years. Dadul was still alive, nor did his illness cause him any suffering whatsoever. He was almost forgotten in his village, except by the relative to whom he had entrusted his fortune, and who scrupulously sent him an abundant supply of stores and clothing. His wife had married again. His son, also married, had no recollection of his father who had left him in childhood. All that he knew was that this father of his was still living in his hermitage . . . a hideous phantom, doubtless, with his flesh eaten away by the terrible leprosy.

Several times this son had been with a servant to replenish his provisions. Not once had he seen him, or tried to speak to him. It was not the custom to do these things. Curling wreaths of smoke ascending had given their silent message . . . the recluse was still alive. . . .

Absorbed in his meditations, just as his relatives and friends were in their material preoccupations, Dadul had forgotten them, as they also had forgotten him.

Jigsjyed had become continually present to him. He had first evoked him in front of his image painted on canvas uttering the ritual words learnt at the time of his "initiation". Then the Terrible One himself had appeared to him and spoken to him at considerable length. Still later, the vision of his form had disappeared and Dadul, instead of the symbolical deity, had glimpsed the very things this deity personified: desire, the thirst after sensation, action, the inevitable destruction that follows it, and desire surviving the ruin of its work, reviving after this work is annihilated and giving rise to new forms immediately destined to die in their turn.

Jigsjyed and the fantastic wife embracing him were not a pair of dreadful lovers, but the world of forms and that of ideas clasping the Void and begetting vain phantoms continually being swallowed up in the Void.

Dadul perceived the breathless panting of countless beings, a prey to the fever of personal existence, to the struggle to preserve that non-existent "self" which Jigsjyed the destroyer ravished from them to make skull necklaces therewith, that "self" which he restored to them with the complicity of his wife: desire, to take it back from them again and again throughout eternity.

The whole universe had entered into the hermitage of Dadul. The "round" of deaths and rebirths, of the life that feeds on death and of the death that absorbs life, this he contemplated with every mouthful he ate, in each idea that rose within him to be effaced in turn by another just born.

Now, one day it happened that a slight seismic shock, or some even simpler cause, shook down a few stones of the wall that enclosed the hermit's dwelling. In the days of his childish fervour, he would have eagerly stopped the breach; now, he was indifferent about it. Other stones fell and the breach widened. One morning, a portion of the crumbling wall gave way, striking the first outer wall and carrying away a corner of it.

The sun's rays entered the cavern, bringing their soothing warmth to Dadul who had been deprived of them for twenty years.

From his couch he beheld the verdant valley, but the spectacle it offered him bore no resemblance to the one he had contemplated in former days. Trees and wind, the rushing water of the stream, the birds cleaving the air: all these seemed to him but so many forms of the universal "Terrible One", the never-ceasing procreator and destroyer.

Seeing him everywhere, Dadul was no longer under the necessity of summoning Jigsjyed in the shadow of a cavern. He went forth to drink from the river.

Away from the stream, sheltered by a natural defence of rocks, spread a tiny pool of still water. Dadul drew near. As he lowered himself, an image rose to meet him. He saw a face he did not know, and whilst looking at it, he remembered what, during all the time he had been in a state of ecstasy, he had quite forgotten: he was Dadul, the leper.

And yet the man who gravely looked at him from the depths of the limpid mirror showed no signs of leprosy.

Amazed, the hermit slipped off his clothes. Naked, in broad daylight, he closely examined himself.

Not the slightest sore was visible, his skin was firm and sound. He felt robust and full of life. . . . The symptoms that had alarmed him so much were those of some other disease which had healed of itself. He had never been leprous at all.

What was he to do? Return home and resume the life of a merchant? The idea made him smile: he had already formed another resolve.

Prostrating himself in the direction of the hermitage where, twenty years previously, he had been initiated into the rites of Jigsjyed, he turned away from his cavern and slowly made his way through the solitary waste.

Tashi Dadul went in quest of the master who would set him on the path of the final initiation, that which leads out of the empire of the "Terrible One", beyond life and death, to inexpressible Nirvâna.

8

THE DIFFERENT TYPES OF
MORALITY

The discipline of constraint, extolled in Tibet by the ordinary religious Masters, is by no means held in honour by initiated mystics. These latter regard the intrinsic worth of a man and the amount of knowledge he possesses as the only elements to be considered in the pursuit of spiritual perfection.

Although, from the social point of view, it is excellent that a man should repress the manifestations of such of his propensities as are incompatible with the well-being of the generality of mankind, this constraint can have no direct result upon his salvation.

However good be the actions he performs when doing violence to his tendencies towards cruelty, hatred, licentiousness or egoism, though momentarily subjugated, these latter nevertheless remain latent within him, ready to spring into being at the first opportunity and to find expression in acts. The might of evil tendencies even increases, at times, as the result of the attention concentrated upon them to bring about their repression.

In addition, the Tibetan mystics believe that the forces driven back into the inmost recesses of the mind or the physical organism, are far from remaining there inactive. In certain cases, they say, there emanate from them occult influences more harmful than would have been the actions they would have generated, had they been allowed to follow their natural bent.

The masters of mysticism do not deny the effects of constraint or coercion. Although they do not use Western words to express these facts, they are well aware that an organ becomes atrophied by lack of exercise, and that a tendency is weakened by persevering repression. For instance, the man who masters his anger and suppresses its manifestations, may in the long run become slow in flying into a passion, or even altogether incapable of doing so.

This *incapacity* is regarded by the Tibetan Masters as a matter for regret. A man *incapable* of committing a crime they look upon as infirm. A man must do good, they declare, because he is influenced by lofty motives. It is not being virtuous to avoid evil actions because one is unable to carry them out.

I have heard expression given to the same theories both in China and in India. In this latter country there is current a humorous anecdote claimed to be authentic. A man, eager to lead a religious life, went to seek a famous *sannyâsin* and entreated him to become his spiritual guide. The *sannyâsin* looked at him steadfastly for a moment, and then suddenly asked him: "Do you know how to lie?" "No," replied his honest interlocutor, "I should never dare to tell a falsehood." "Then go and learn," replied the holy man. "When you are able to tell a lie, come back. Then I will see what may fittingly be taught you concerning the spiritual life." This was said in no jesting spirit. Incapacity really is debility – not a virtue.

For this reason the method which weakens or suppresses any material manifestation whatsoever, while the feeling that gave rise to it remains undestroyed, is considered useless, even harmful to spiritual growth.

What is judged necessary is a sort of transmutation of the substance which makes up the disciple. The forces existing within him should by no means be destroyed, rather should they be methodically directed along suitable channels. The *naljorpa* beginner should learn to regulate or to combine the antagonistic tendencies which he discovers within him, with a view to obtaining the desired results.

This "combination" of opposite forces the clever adept of the "Short Path" doctrine practises, even when he yields to his passions, whether in order to make a psychic experiment or merely to allow himself some kind of inferior enjoyment, such as revenge or lust.

In this last case, the aim of the *naljorpa* is to avoid, either partially or entirely, the harmful results of his evil deeds.

Such a way of sinning skilfully cannot fail to appear odd, even offensive, to many of my readers, but this is not the case with people who, instead of seeing before them the commandments of a God whom they conceive as being in their own likeness, consider nothing but the law of cause and effect, with its manifold combinations.

Perhaps the philosophers of Tibet themselves conceived these ideas, or perhaps they borrowed them from India. However it be, educated India professed similar opinions on this point, as we see in the famous work entitled: *The Questions of King Milinda.*

The following is the passage in question:

The king asked Nâgasena, a famous Buddhist philosopher:

"Who has the greater demerit – he who sins consciously or he who sins inadvertently?"

"He who sins inadvertently, O King, has the greater demerit."

"In that case, reverend Sir, we shall punish doubly any of our family or our court who do wrong unintentionally."

"But what do you think, O King? If a man were to seize hold intentionally of a fiery mass of metal glowing with heat, and another were to seize hold of it unintentionally, which would be the more burnt?"

"He who did not know what he was doing?"

"Well, it is just the same with the man who does wrong."

It is fitting to give the term "demerit" its Buddhic significance. We are not concerned with disobedience to a divine Creator who judges with feelings similar to our own. Certainly he, like the king, will have all sorts of good reasons for seeming indulgent to the man who fails him inadvertently, but the example given by the king does not apply to the question, that is why Nâgasena opposes it with another.

The man who knows that he is about to touch a piece of burning metal will be able to take such precautions as are likely to mitigate the natural effect of a contact between the human skin and red-hot iron. He will plunge his hands in water, wrap it in water-soaked cloths, or employ some other artifice. The ignorant man will apply his hand to the burning metal without taking any precaution whatsoever, and will experience cruel suffering.

So do there exist, for certain vices of a material or a moral order, antidotes susceptible of mitigating their evil consequences. The initiate who has been warned is likely to make use of them.

In making profession of these theories, Tibetans reveal their profound faith in that discerning skill which has given rise to the picturesque and very characteristic proverb: "He who knows how to go the right way to work will live comfortably even in hell." Therefore, how much more easily will he succeed in protecting himself from the drawbacks of his own nature.

Blind and mad, say the Tibetan philosophers, is the vulgar[1] man who, carried away by his passions, derogates from the moral laws decreed by certain Sages to guide the masses of humanity. He will purchase an ephemeral pleasure at the cost of prolonged suffering.

The morality of the initiate, however, is not that of the masses.

Although rigid rules, applied indiscriminately in all circumstances, cause a great deal of harm, according to Tibetan ascetics, a complete absence of rules would probably cause greater harm. Consequently one must not turn aside feeble minds from the observance of moral codes.

The enlightened man, however, has nothing to do with this; his morality consists in the wise choice he is capable of making between what is useful and what is harmful, according to circumstances.

The doctrines of the "Mystic Path" admit neither of Good nor of Evil in themselves. The degree in which an action is useful marks its place in the scale of moral values. "Utility", in this category of *naljorpas*, almost always has the meaning of goodness, charity, help to those who suffer, or destruction of the cause of suffering.

To lie may become a sacred duty if it is a question of saving the life of a man hounded down by assassins. To rob a wealthy miser in order to feed those who are dying of hunger is by no means evil. And if the *naljorpa* foresees that he will be imprisoned or beaten in consequence of his action, and yet, notwithstanding this knowledge of the risk he incurs, commits

---

[1]Vulgar in the sense of being stupid, unenlightened. In this connection the term "childish" is often used in Tibetan works.

the theft from pity to those who suffer, then he is a saint.

It is interesting to bear witness to the fact that this way of regarding things, which will be dubbed revolutionary by many, forms the basis of many ancient Buddhist stories, the heroes of which give alms of things which do not belong to them.

Lamaists admit that even murder may be a good action, but the murderer must be actuated by motives devoid of all personal interest. He should not hate the one he wants to kill, and he must be capable of transmuting into a beneficent force the evil-tending energy which animates the one he would destroy. If he cannot do this, he ought, when committing the murder, to ally himself with someone who has this power.

It is this transmutation which is exoterically and popularly described as "sending the spirit" of the murdered being into an abode of bliss.

The praises lavished in the old legends upon Lamas or heroes like Gesar, slayers of demoniacal giants,[1] are based on these theories.

There is one historical fact, the political murder of Langdharma in the ninth century by a Lama, which clearly shows the Lamaist point of view in this matter.

The king had returned to the ancient religion of Tibet; he was protecting its followers and endeavouring to extirpate Buddhism from his States.

The Lamaist chronicles, which alone can give us information regarding this sovereign, depict him under the forbidding aspect of a persecutor, but it is possible that the Lama clergy, who had now become greedy and ambitious, may have had as their principal grievance against Langdharma the opposition he offered to the encroachments of the monks

[1] It may be believed that those of whom the legends have made demons were very probably, in the case of Gesar, chiefs of enemy tribes.

upon the temporal power of the king.

However it be, the murder of this Tibetan Julian the Apostate is even nowadays extolled, and the religious assassin is an important character of the "Mysteries" which are mimed and danced in the monasteries. The Lama did not have recourse to occult means for the murder of his victim, as is often the case with the heroes of legends. He disguised himself as a dancing clown and went out to give a performance in the court of the palace, in order to induce the king to come out on to the balcony. Immediately he appeared, the would-be dancer let fly an arrow at him which he had concealed in one of his flowing sleeves. Then he took to flight on a horse which accomplices held in readiness for him.

In such a circumstance – as in any other in which a murder may bring about relief or deliverance of oppressed human beings – the truly compassionate man should become a murderer, even though his action leads him to endure the worst of torments for millions of years in one or other of the purgatories. "Compassion and service in the first place" is the motto of the initiate at this stage of his spiritual journey.

How an act that is considered good may, on the other hand, have an unhappy rebirth as its consequences, will doubtless appear amazing and illogical. The Lamaists have many explanations of such a thing. Retributive justice, as applied in our own lands, is here inapplicable. One might rather compare the case of a "murderer from compassion" with that of a doctor who contracts an infectious disease because of his devotion to a patient. Contagion of a subtler nature is said to threaten the man who commits the supremely terrible action of taking life. By doing so, he creates within himself certain occult affinities capable of attracting him to an unhappy rebirth. In contradistinction, however, to the ordinary criminal by whose side he may live during his new life, the "murdered from compassion" will still be animated by noble feelings and ever capable, even in purgatory, of devotion and altruism, just as a doctor, afflicted with leprosy or cancer, will remain intelligent and often capable of pursuing his scientific studies. This comparison to a doctor, after all, is approximate and far-fetched, as are all comparisons. What we must remember is, according to the initiates, that unlawful acts - like contagious diseases – distil poison. They declare, however, that there are psychic and other "antiseptics" which enable one to guard against infection.

I have heard the same idea expressed by adepts of the Japanese sect Nichiren. One of them, belonging to the religious order, said to me: "It is not sufficient to abstain from doing evil, evil must also be fought and maleficent beings destroyed." It is fitting to note that, according to the Buddhists, the evil being who is killed is not condemned to an eternal hell. Possibly the "accident" that befalls him acts as a salutary spur, urging him to a better course. At all events, the Lamaists entertain this hope and discourse complaisantly on the many wonderful effects of that peculiar kind of charity. Not only, they say, does it save innocent victims but, arresting the course of the criminal's misdeeds, it prevents him from sinking more deeply into crime. Perhaps it will arouse in his mind at the moment of death a salutary repentance, a desire for redemption which will bear him to rebirth armed with nobler tendencies. Even, if his perverse mind is incapable of this effort, the all-compassionate murderer may substitute itself for him in its accomplishment.

How excellent! . . . Too excellent, perhaps. The declivity is a dangerous one. I imagine that certain savage inquisitors must have based upon similar opinions their charitable zeal regarding the heretics they burned alive. Such opinions are not authorised by primitive Buddhism.

As has just been said, the man who transgresses the ordinary moral law should be completely disinterested and obtain no personal benefit from his transgression.

And yet, in theory, those who have reached the spiritual heights to which the mystic Path leads, are said to be freed from this latter restriction. The direction of their conduct is left entirely to their wisdom. What is expected of them is an absolute impartiality which will make them look upon their needs with the same detachment as they look upon the needs of others.

They are not altogether forbidden to enjoy a personal benefit, for, in the case of certain superior individuals, this benefit may serve some object of general interest.

An example of this as applying to Westerners might be given by quoting the case of a scientist who, placed in comfortable and fortunate circumstances, might enable the whole world to benefit by discoveries or inventions which he would not have been able to bring about if he had lived a poor man.

This part of the Path becomes more and more slippery, and the masters do not fail to warn the aspirant *naljorpas* of the dangers incurred by those who have not adequately overcome the desires engendered by attachment to "self". It is commonly declared that if the disciple does not succeed in attaining enlightenment and a passionless mental state, when he enters this path he becomes a demon.

To sum up, there is one law which dominates the many – sometimes paradoxical – forms which the Good may assume in the initiate's eyes: he must combat suffering, never be the cause of it, he must bring it to pass that those he afflicts shall be benefited by the very pain he is compelled to inflict upon them, so that great numbers may profit thereby. The problem is a difficult one: simple goodness or love of a justice based on incorrect conceptions is incapable of solving it. The initiates of Tibet are convinced of this and declare that intelligence developed by prolonged spiritual training is necessary if one would attain to the perfection of the bodhisattvas,[1] whose very thought and deeds contain nothing harmful to other beings.

And yet morality under whatsoever aspect – even when interpreted as wisdom – belongs to that lower part of the "Mystic Path" where activity is still regarded as the performance of physical and mental actions.

Technically this stage is called *chös kyi töspa*,[2] "religious or virtuous activity".

In proportion as the disciple advances in introspection, the more clearly does he understand how futile is activity which attempts to turn aside the course of causes and effects by basing one's reasons on short-sighted perceptions and equally short-sighted sentiments.

The stage called *tös tal*,[3] "the rejection of activity", is then reached. The mystic understands that what really matters is not *to do*, but *to be*.

The following comparison will conduce to an understanding of the mind of the masters of mysticism better than will any kind of explanation:

The sun – one of them said to me – does not work. It does not think: "I am about to send my rays upon this particular man to warm him, upon this particular field to ripen the barley, upon this particular country so that its inhabitants may enjoy the light." But because it is the sun, warm and light-giving in its essence, it illumines, and gives warmth and life to all beings.

It is just the same with a Changchub Semspa, a superior individuality that is all intelligence, wisdom, and goodness.

---

[1] In Tibetan: *Changchub semspa*.
[2] Written *tchos kyi spros pa*.
[3] Written *spros bral*. This stage is also called *tös med*, written *spros med*.

Because he is made of this marvellous substances, the beneficent energy he releases radiates upon and envelops all beings, from the highest gods to the most wretched dwellers in purgatory.

Nevertheless, this sublime rôle should not be coveted by the disciple advancing along the "Mystic Path".

Whereas Mahâyâna Buddhism regards as the noblest of religious aspirations that expressed in the vow to become a powerful Changchub Semspa, capable of working for the happiness of all beings, this desire is approved only in the lower degrees of the "Mystic Path". It is afterwards rejected as being tinged with attachment to individual life, with belief in the "self".

If he gives expression to a vow at all, the disciple who has attained to the higher initiations will formulate it impersonally: "May a Changchub Semspa or a Buddha arise for the good of all beings!" not "May I myself become a Changchub Semspa!"

The one essential condition for reaching the higher degrees is the complete renunciation of "self" in every aspect. It has been said: "Nirvâna is not for those who desire it, because the very thing of which Nirvâna consists is the utter absence of desire."

The path certainly does not yet end here. The *naljorpa*, however, is now supposed to have arrived before the mystic peaks. Rules, practices, and rites are all left behind. There remains only meditation, which the masters compare to a free-meandering course over summits bathed in air that is delightfully pure and fresh.

On these vast spiritual highlands whose pallid reflection in matter is seen in the enchanting solitudes of Tibet, the track ceases to be visible. We must renounce following the steps of the fully liberated mystic who has glimpsed the absolute freedom of Nirvâna. "As the track of birds through the air, his path is alike difficult to trace."[1]

And if one of them turns in our direction, consenting to unveil to us the secret of his contemplations, he is soon checked by the impossibility of relating his mystic experiences. It is to these that allusion is made in the classic phrase of the Prajñâpâramitâ:[2] *Mre sam djöd med*:[3] "I should like to speak but . . . words fail me."

---

[1] *Dhammapada*, 93.
[2] The philosophical treatise attributed to Nâgârjuna; the Tibetan name of this work is *Shes rab kyi pharol tu byin pa*.
[3] Written *smras bsam rjod med*.

9

THE CULTIVATION OF ATTENTION[1]

The principal aim of Buddhism is to put an end to suffering and so its adepts are offered a course of mental culture designed to lead them to this eminently desirable end.

This programme implies, first of all, and as a principle, the necessity of holding views that are true, for, indeed, if views are based upon erroneous beliefs then even with the best intentions the results obtained will be unfortunate.

Real knowledge is a highly subjective thing since knowledge which others can impart to us is not, in effect, real for us. Real knowledge is that which is born of our flesh and our spirit, that which is due to the experience of our senses coupled with reasoning. Valid and efficient knowledge results from observations whose correctness has been confirmed by repeated proof. It follows from this that the True View which results from right knowledge can be obtained only by the assiduous practice of vigilant attention.

To what must attention be directed? It must be directed to all manner of things; to the material facts we discover

[1]This chapter has been written from notes made by the Lama Yongden.

around us, to the mental activity we discern in others; concepts, opinions, passions, in all their forms and manifestations. However, this continual attention must be, above all, directed towards ourselves.

We must watch carefully our reactions to the various contacts made by our senses and our spirit with our environment. We must catch, as it were upon the wing, the various manifestations of our physical and mental activity, hold them and interrogate them. "Whence did you come?" "What engendered you?" "What are your parents?" "What, farther away than your parents, can one discover in the jumble of your ancestors?"

A problem often set to their disciples by the Masters of the Sect of Meditation[1] is framed thus: "What visage did you possess before your father and mother were born?"

The Zen adepts say that this problem may refer to the

---

[1] The sect of "Meditation" (*dhyâna*, in Chinese *Ts'an* and in Japanese *Zen*) is said to have been introduced into China by Bodhidharma, the son of a southern Indian prince, about A.D. 520. Japanese Zen, however, owes its origin – about the year 1200 – to Yosai, who studied in China for several years. Originally this sect taught that introspective meditation alone can lead us to Knowledge and that such illuminating Knowledge may suddenly burst upon the spirit as the result of a psychic shock which forces us to perceive a truth which has always been present before us but which we did not notice. The Zen Masters seek to provoke this shock by setting their disciples problems which appear to be absurd or by uttering in their disciples' presence statements absolutely contrary to common sense and to reality as it can be ordinarily observed. Bodhidharma retired to a hermitage in the province of Honan near to the Shaolin *sse* or monastery. Tradition has it that he died in his hermitage after spending nine years in meditation. In 1917 Alexandra David-Neel and the Lama Yongden stayed at the Shaolin *sse*. Before this both of them had lived for nearly a year in the Tofu Kuji, the great monastery of the Rinzai Zen sect in Kyôto and had also passed some time in other Zen monasteries, especially in Korea. The sobriety of the original doctrines of Bodhidharma has undergone profound modification and the modern adepts

succession of existences, to what in popular language are called "reincarnations" and then again the problem may refer to the origin of the appearance of those phenomena that constitute the world.

But without losing ourselves in the formulation of hypotheses, fruits of our imagination (a vain task against which Buddhism warns us) we must learn to untangle the skein of the multifarious causes whose temporary contact has brought about effects which we can observe in ourselves and around about us.

These causes did not meet and mingle by mere chance. They themselves were subjected to the influence of other causes which guided them.

These directing causes are not, moreover, solely exterior, they may be due to the peculiar nature of the elements operating in the aggregate – that is to say, in this case, our own person itself.

Buddhists are often heard to speak of the "memory"

of Ts'an (that is Zen) have adopted ritualistic practices and classified and codified the "problems" (*koans*) which in early times, were proposed spontaneously as circumstances suggested.

The sects derived from the Dhyâna School (Ts'an and Zen) are numerous both in China and in Japan. The most important of the Japanese Zen sects are the Rinzai, imported from China by Master Rinzai in 1191, the Sôtô sect brought in by Yôsai about 1200, and the sect founded later on by Obaku. The Rinzai sect has the reputation of being the most intellectual, the most aristocratic while the Sôtô sect has by far the greatest number of followers. The Obaku sect is not very numerous.

At the time of my stay in Japan the numbers of religious masters teaching the doctrines of the three Zen Schools were approximately as follows: Sôtô 9,576 – Rinzai, 4,528 – Obaku 840. This information was given me by Professor Kaiten Nukariya.

In recent years various doctrines, under the name of Zen, have spread in Europe and America, but these doctrines have hardly any resemblance to those of the Ts'an and Zen sects as taught by the Chinese and Japanese masters of those Buddhist schools of thought.

which an individual may retain concerning his former incarnations.

Numerous writings, of the *Jataka* type, describe in detail episodes in the successive lives of human, divine or even animal figures, which are stated to have been the Buddha preparing himself, during the course of his various existences, to attain the degree of moral and mental perfection and of acuity of perception indispensable for the production of spiritual illumination.

Many eminent Buddhists have been furnished with "genealogies" of this kind. In Tibet the Lamas known as *Tulkus* (whom foreigners call, most improperly, "Living Buddhas") are held to be links in the chain of incarnations of a single person. Indeed, according to this belief, each one of us, before his birth into this world, has accomplished a long journey of transmigration from body to body and sometimes from world to world. This belief which is held by most of the ignorant Buddhists is, however, in flagrant contradiction with the fundamental principles of Buddhism. The belief is borrowed from the Hindu idea concerning the *Jiva*, the principle of individuality that undergoes transmigration from body to body.

The famed Indian epic, the *Bhagavadgîtâ*, offers a vivid illustration of this doctrine:

"Just as a man puts off his old clothing to put on new, so also 'that which is incarnated' (*dehi*) puts off his old bodies to assume new ones."

How, we may ask, could such a conception find place in a teaching which proclaims the transitory nature of all associations of elements and which denies in these any permanent principle at all? *Jiva, Dehi,* soul, spirit, *ego*, or whatever name we may choose to give it?

Anicca Anatta, impermanence, absence of *ego* every-where, in all things, that is the Buddhist creed.

This creed is not presented by Buddhism as emanating from any revelation but as the fruit of a discovery, of a knowl-edge acquired by means of Attention, or sustained Investigation. It was by examination, by reflection and medi-tation that the Buddha attained spiritual Illumination, and each one of us may attain it by using the same means.

What then is the "rebirth" as it is conceived by well-informed and enlightened Buddhists? It is made up of the persistent activity of an energy that is manifested in different forms, by virtue of a combination of causes and effects.

What I think of as "myself" as "my very self" as a unit, as a person, as an *ego*, is, in reality, an unstable aggregate of ele-ments, an aggregate of "lives", one may say, deriving from various sources and momentarily united and active.

The activity of the various elements entering into the composition of the aggregate is not always exercised in co-operation, nor always at the same time. While some may seem numbed, the vitality of others may be manifested with vio-lence, some tend towards one end, while others tend to a different end or even to one diametrically opposed. Hence result mental conflicts, those rending divisions in our being when we feel urged to action by instincts, by desires that are conflicting and contradictory.

Sustained attention, perspicacious investigation will show us that we are not a unit but a plurality, that we shelter, temporarily, guests of varying origins, come from all points of the universe and as the lengthy consequences of intermingled causes and effects, and without our being able to assign to them any original starting-point.

It is written in the *Samyutta Nikâya*:

"Unknowable is the beginning of that long pilgrimage of beings enveloped in ignorance and who, spurred on by desire, carry on the round of rebirths and of lives renewed without ceasing."

Buddhism does not explain the origin of the world and of sentient beings. Buddhism is addressed to men who reject mythological tales and empty speculations regarding the origin of the universe. Indeed, it would seem that in this matter of the cause of the universe's origin – and in a more restricted field, of that of the appearance of life on our earth – Western scientists are of much the same opinion as the sages of India, those who expressed themselves in the *Samyutta Nikâya* that we have just cited, and those who long before had sung in the hymns of the *Rigveda*:

"Who knoweth whence this creation has come. . . . He whose throne is higher than the Heavens, may know and may not know."

If Buddhism leaves on one side the problem of a First Cause, nevertheless, the Buddhist is exhorted to discern the nature of the elements which make up that he calls his "self". He is encouraged to follow up, as far as possible, the line of causes and effects which have contributed to the constitution of these elements and have led to their momentary union. Buddhists are recommended to watch, with sustained attention, the behaviour of these diverse elements, their friendly or unfriendly relations with one another, the help that they give each other mutually and the conflicts which occur between them.

A clear view of these various activities which occur within him will explain to the observer his changes of temper, his revulsions of opinion, and the diversity of the acts which thus ensue.

In truth each supposed *ego* is a meeting-place where jostles about a crowd that comes and goes continually by many roads, for members of this crowd are constantly on the move to join other crowds at other meeting-places of universal life.

It is an excellent thing to attain this vision of union in diversity, to feel *others* live in ourselves and to perceive *ourselves* living in others.

Thus *myself* and *yourself* have lived in interdependence without perceptible beginnings and thus we shall continue to exist without any conceivable end. This is the same, on the human scale, as eternal life made up of continual deaths and continual rebirths.

Should we be content with this conception – however justified it may be – and consider it as the expression of Truth – with a capital "T"?

A reply to this question must lead us into that realm of Buddhism whose inhabitants acknowledge the leadership of Nâgârjuna and other sages of his school, that is to say those who affirm that such thinkers are the most faithful interpreters of the Buddha's teaching.

We must distinguish, they say, two sorts of truth – relative and absolute truth. Of these two kinds only the former, relative truth, is accessible to us. It is a truth on the human scale, for beings such as we are, furnished with the means of perception we possess, that is to say our five senses applied to material objects and our spirit applied to abstract ideas.

If there is no absolute Truth or if it is inaccessible to us – which comes to the same thing as far as we are concerned – can we speak of an absolute Reality? Obviously not.

"Like visions seen in a dream, so must we regard all things."

These are the closing words of the "Book of Transcendent Knowledge" or rather the "Book of the Passing beyond Knowledge" the *Prajñâpâramitâ* (in Tibetan *Shésrab kyi pharol tu phyinpa*).

The philosophical Buddhist school founded on the teaching of Nâgârjuna and of the *Prajñâpâramitâ* written by him, teaches that our world and the furnishings of material objects and mental concepts with which we provide it, is made up of structures with which our spirit is continually occupied. These are the *samskâras* (in Tibetan *du chéd*). The word *samskâra* means an "assemblage" or "structure". *Samskâras* are denounced in the most ancient Buddhist texts as fed by ignorance and as instigators of suffering.

One of the main principles which the Tibetan spiritual masters endeavour to inculcate upon their pupils is "Do not imagine", that is "Do not indulge in the play of mental building, of making edifices among the clouds, with the clouds" – theories and dogmas resting in the void.

Before the time of the Buddha, the Indians used already to say, figuratively:

"The world is the dream of Brahmâ, when Brahmâ ceases to dream the world disappears."

For intellectual Buddhists of the Mahâyâna School, the world is not the dream of some fabled Brahmâ, but our own dream, the dream of each one of us.

Each one of us fabricates, continuously, in his spirit, images of the world with its many aspects which, so it seems to him, surrounds him and in which he sees himself playing a part as he may do in a dream. The world is not *outside* of us but *in* us.

Such being the case, the problem of a First Clause for the

Universe (its beginnings taking place in time) no longer exists. Our universe begins anew at every moment with our thoughts which weave illusory shapes "like images seen in a dream" as Nâgârjuna wrote.

"It will be a very difficult thing for men to understand the extinction of the *samskâras*, quietude, Nirvâna."[1]

No single term in all the Buddhist vocabulary has been more misunderstood by non-Buddhists than the word *Nirvâna*. We are told that it means the annihilation of the individual, the annihilation of "self". But how could Buddhists speak of the annihilation of the *ego* when they categorically deny its existence?

The "destruction" in question is that of fanciful, unreal conceptions spun by an imagination fed on erroneous views. Fed by ignorance, depending upon ignorance, buttressed by ignorance, as is said in the canonical Buddhist texts.

Vigilant attention is just what can reveal the inanity of these conceptions, eliminate them and prevent other and similar conceptions from taking their place.

In this way will be attained that which is beyond what makes up the world, that is to say the suppression of daydreams and an awakening; that is Nirvâna.

He who, while keeping the appearance of playing a part in this world of illusion nonetheless considers it with the serenity conferred by a realisation of its true nature – that of "images seen as in a dream of which he himself is the creator" – he who has dissipated, by means of profound investigation, the false notions which he had cherished concerning a permanent "self", needs not to die in order to reach *Nirvâna*. He has

---

[1] A saying that is attributed, in the *Mahavagga*, to the Buddha.

attained it while living, as did the Buddha and as have done many of his disciples.

For such a man death is not what it seems to most men who are held in bondage to their own mental conceptions. Death has ceased to exist for him who has reached Nirvâna because he has ceased to create for it a reality, just as we endow with reality the events we live through in a dream.

It is written in the *Dhammapada*:

"He who regards the world with the same look as one regards a bubble, he indeed is capable of no longer seeing the realm of death."

In another passage we can read:

"Attention is the path that leads to freedom from death; lack of reflection leads to death. Those who are attentive do not die. Those who lack attention are already as though they were dead."

10

COSMIC CONSCIOUSNESS

The idea that a kind of "memory" is stored up in the objects that surround us is rather widespread in Tibet. According to the degree of intelligence and learning of those who profess this doctrine it may tend to be expressed in a more or less puerile fashion or, again, tend to resemble abstruse theories derived from those concerning the *alâya vijñâna* ("storing up of consciousness") in Mahâyâna philosophy.

I should like to mention, first of all, some facts which seem to me significant as showing how there may arise in the minds of ingenuous men an idea that material objects, just in the same way as human beings, can become efficient under the influence of impressions they have felt and recorded.

During the time that I lived on the northern border of Sikkim, on the last crest of the Himâlaya and opposite the little Tibetan frontier-town called Kampa Dzong, on several occasions I passed by the entrance to a very narrow valley, almost a ravine. Its appearance was sombre and exceptionally wild. The local population held that the canyon was haunted by demons which, from time to time, would assume the form of a formidable dog that would make as though to attack passers-by. The mountaineers would defend themselves with their sticks and recite pious invocations addressed to the goddess Dolma who protects travellers. Then the dog would disappear and that would be all. Nevertheless, the story was that the dog really had bitten a passing pilgrim, though the tale was not confirmed.

But that a dog did sometimes appear seemed to be quite certain. Plenty of people had seen it though they could not explain why it should live in such an extraordinary place since the spot where it showed itself was far away (over thirty miles) from any village or encampment. Again, it was always the same dog that had appeared for a number of years since the accounts given by those who had seen it agreed as to the look and behaviour of the animal.

That apparitions should have been seen in this valley was, in itself, not particularly surprising. Comparable happenings had been related of other places. In one of them, especially, the phenomena were auditive. From time to time an invisible, impalpable flute player was heard.

Various opinions were current concerning these facts. I collected a number of these statements. Here are a few of them.

One of my interlocutors said to me:

"There must have happened, in this place, some incident like that seen by passers-by. A dog must have attacked a man. Probably because of the power diffused by the great fear that the man underwent, the scene became, as it were, imprinted on the rocks and soil of the valley. Some people are able to discern such images and take them for actions that are occurring at the time these men pass by."

I made no comment on this opinion although the man who pronounced it shared the views of many other people. A believe in the images of scenes or persons of the past being stamped upon objects is more widespread than is often thought.

Another man I talked to said:

"The incident must have been one that has been told, and retold for a very long time so that it has become rooted in the memory of the local inhabitants. When they pass by the valley they remember the story about the menacing dog so that their thoughts materialise, so to speak, the shape and the behaviour of the dog which then plays the part he does in the stories they have heard. This re-enacting of the original incident, although quite subjective, is not lacking in efficiency for its action upon the surroundings induces them to assist in the production of new visions of the angry dog."

A Lama of the Dzogschénpas sect expressed the opinion which is current among the adepts of the idealistic school:

"There is neither demon nor dog, although some people, no doubt, see both. One of my monks once passed that way. He did not belong to the region and had never heard of the story that a dog would appear in the valley. Nevertheless, he did see the dog and it looked as though it were going to attack him. Then he recalled the story of Milarespa[1] finding demons who had taken up their abode in the cavern that served him as a hermitage and admonishing himself in these words: 'It is really not worth while, my poor Mila, to have spent so many years in meditation and to have sat at the feet of a most eminent Master, and then to believe in the existence of demons. Do you now know that they exist only in your own spirit that ponders on the superstitious beliefs of the ignorant and those you yourself held before

[1] This story is related on pp. 229-30 in the chapter on the "Tibetan Intelligentsia".

your enlightenment?' Thereupon, Milarespa began to laugh and said to the evil spirits: 'Take your ease, settle down here, I know that you are nothing but an illusion.' Whereupon the diabolic shapes vanished.

"My monk, being convinced that no real dog could possibly be seen in such a place, imitated Milarespa and with the same success."

This explanation seemed to satisfy the Lama, but I wanted to hear some other explanations.

Why did this *trapa*[1] who was quite ignorant of the local beliefs about meeting with a dog in this particular valley, see there a dog rather than anything else?

I got some more – and varied – replies.

One of those I interrogated rejected, out of hand, the idea that images could have become impressed, in a quasi-material fashion on the rocks and soil of the valley, but he suggested that occult influences originating in the feelings of terror experienced by the man who, at one time long before, really had been attacked by a dog, persisted in the area of the valley and encouraged, in the case of "receptive" individuals, the vision of what had happened in bygone times.

"All the cases of comparable phenomena," said he, "occurring in definite places, can be attributed to causes of this sort. We are immersed in currents of subtle powers. Each one of our movements, each one of our thoughts is like a stone thrown into the water and there produces ripples, these ripples, that are movement, set up other movements whose effects we feel and they make us see visions, arouse thoughts in us, etc."

Little by little, by means of these different opinions, there was an approach to the idea of the preservation of the past, to

[1] *Trapa* (written *grapa*) a member of the inferior Tibetan clergy.

the theories derived from those of the *Alâya Vijñâna* ("the storehouse of consciousness") or Cosmic Consciousness.

The world which we can, generally, perceive, I heard said, is only a minute part of the world in which we are plunged, to which we belong. Occasionally, some of us get a glimpse of that sphere which is almost always closed to us although its action upon us is constant, continuous.

Nothing disappears, nothing is blotted out, nothing is annihilated. To believe that what we call the "past" has ceased to exist, or that the traces it has left in our memory are immaterial and dead, is an error. The past acts constantly upon the present; it is living in the present, it is not relegated.

That depository of consciousness or memories called the *Alâya Vigñâna* must not be thought of as situated somewhere in space, outside the sphere in which we move and live. About each one of us is produced, at every moment, a storing up of the energy released by our actions and our thoughts, while, at the same time, there is poured into us, in various ways, the energy that gives rise to our acts and our thoughts, the energy that never ceases to create the worlds.

Some believe that this continuity of contributions to the storing up of "memory-energy" and discharge of this "memory-energy" must bring about the repetition of past events.

Some Indians regard such a repetition in a way that seems somewhat crude and arid.

Once when I was at Benares and sitting in a garden with five pundits one of them said to me, "One day the five of us will find ourselves back in this garden just as we are now. The garden will be exactly the same as it is today. We shall speak of the things we are discussing now, we shall use the same words."

This sort of "eternal return" seemed quite unacceptable

to those scholarly Tibetans to whom I repeated the words of the pundit in Benares. Supposing, they said to me, our world contains six classes of beings[1] that is to say six distinct and different worlds, as is set forth in our ancient religious books, which are, so to speak, imprisoned behind impassable barriers, the infinite variety of combinations to which they must give rise if they meet, will produce an infinite diversity of different effects. A rigorous and complete repetition of the disposition of the elements which have produced past events may be considered as practically impossible.

And then we may consider that the "memories" proceeding from physical or psychical activities cannot be thought of as possessing a stable and individual character. These "memories" may be compared with groups, with whirlwinds of heterogeneous forces all efficient according to their proper nature and in perpetual movement. It is as such that they rush into the common fund of the universe's "memory-consciousness-energy".

My Tibetan friends considered this "storehouse" as fed not only by the activity of our world but also by that produced in the six other worlds they recognise. With this view as a starting-point, those who are more instructed than they are could enlarge the communion of the "six worlds" and apply it to a really universal communion.

In fact, is not this reservoir, or storehouse, the efficient centre of continual arrivals and departures. Is it not the Eternal Existence?

However, it is wise to remind oneself that this concept is like all others, a construction of our spirit and is valid only for beings whose mental and physical faculties are like our own. It

[1] i.e. the gods, the non-gods (roughly Titans), men, non-men, genii, fairies, demons, etc., beings inhabiting the worlds where sorrow reigns ("hells" but which do not hold their victims for ever).

is certain, also, that as long as we remain imprisoned within an instinctive sentiment that leads us to think of ourselves as distinct "selves", individuals existing by themselves as distinguished from other individuals, the "Universal Life" can be for us nothing more than a subject for discourse. To be conscious of *being* Universal Life is, perhaps, to possess the secret of Enlightenment, that is Nirvâna.

But to "be conscious", we may say, implies that we still feel a "self", a distinct *ego*. Is not that an operation of the spirit, a sensation enveloped in duality?

We must, no doubt, think of the state of transcendental *samâdhi* in which there is, we are told, neither consciousness nor lack of consciousness. That is to say that this state is indescribable, nay, even inconceivable. We must, then, be content to dream of Cosmic Consciousness. Still, it is very possible that some dreams may be the portals of reality.

11

THE TEACHING OF TIBETAN MYSTICS

In order to enable readers to form for themselves some idea of the instruction which the religious teachers of Tibet impart to their disciples, I will here add a number of maxims attributed to the famous Lama Dagpo Lha Dje who was the third in direct succession of the masters of the line of the Kahgyud-pas, the most important of the schools claiming to possess a traditional oral teaching. The Tibetan word Kahgyud means "a line of precepts".

The philosopher Tilopa, represented as a sort of Hindu Diogenes, is the ancestor of this line. His disciple, Narota, who taught at the celebrated Buddhist university of Nalanda (in the tenth century) had amongst his pupils the Tibetan Marpa. The latter introduced into his land the doctrines of Tilopa which he had received from Narota. These he passed on to his disciple the poet-ascetic Milarespa (eleventh century), who in turn imparted them to his two eminent disciples Dagpo Lha Dje and Reschungpa.[1]

This latter, in imitation of his Master Milarespa, lived the life of an anchorite, and Dagpo Lha Dje continued the

[1] Regarding Tilopa and his disciples see *With Mystics and Magicians in Tibet*.

line of the spiritual sons of Tilopa still in existence. This is now represented by the chiefs of several branches that have sprung from disciples of Dagpo Lha Dje, the chief one being the Grand Lama of the Karma-Kahgyud who lives in the monastery of Tolung Cherpug, two days' march from Lhasa.

Dagpo Lha Dje is the author of a considerable number of mystical and philosophical works. The maxims I have translated appear to have been gleaned from these works in order to form a collection originally intended for the lay devotees and the monks, disciples of the Lamas of the sect of the Kahgyud-pas. They are frequently uttered by word of mouth, and the disciples who have learned them by heart sometimes write them down, the better to remember them. These small manuscripts are then communicated to other monks or to pious laymen who may copy them and put them also into circulation. Nevertheless, printed texts of these maxims are in existence. They differ from one another in detail but the main principles of the teaching do not change.

The style of this kind of treatise is extremely concise. The clear-cut form of the maxims is calculated to rivet the attention and to stamp them on the memory. Unfortunately it is impossible to attempt a literal translation of them; this would be incomprehensible. The use of explanatory phrases is inevitable, though these largely tone down the distinctive flavour of the original text.

§

For the use of those desirous of escaping from the round of successive existences are here set forth certain of the precepts of the master Dagpo Lha Dje, spiritual heir of the Sages of the sect of the Kahgyud-pas. Let us render homage to this line of instructors whose glory is immaculate, whose virtues are inexhaustible as the ocean, and who enfold all beings, past, present, and future throughout the universe, in their infinite benevolence.

§

He who aspires to be delivered from death, to attain to spiritual enlightenment, the state of the Buddha, ought first to meditate upon the following points.

Having come to birth as a human being, to squander this human life by employing it in the performance of unreasonable or evil actions, and to die after living a common ordinary life, would be a matter of regret.

In this life, the duration of which is so brief, it would be a matter of regret to yield to vain ambition and to allow one's mind to wallow in the slime of the world's illusions.

A wise master being a guide to liberation, it would be a matter of regret for us to separate from him before attaining enlightenment.

Our rules of conduct and our moral engagements being the vehicle which carries us towards emancipation, it would be a matter of regret if our passions led us to transgress against the former and to break the latter.

The inner light having shone within us, it would be a matter of regret if we allowed it to flicker out amid trivial preoccupations.

It would be a matter of regret if, after coming to know the precious doctrine of the Sages, we were to sell it for our livelihood or for vile profit, to those incapable of appreciating it.

As all beings are our relatives towards whom we have incurred obligations, it would be a matter of regret were we to feel antipathy or indifference towards them.

§

After attentively and impartially examining one's own nature, faculties and powers, one must trace for oneself a prudent line of conduct.

Entire confidence in his spiritual guide is indispensable for a disciple, as also are perseverance and energy; therefore, being well aware of the qualities required of a master and the faults from which he must be exempt, it is fitting to seek a spiritual guide who is worthy of confidence.

A keen intellect, firm faith, steady perseverance in the application of one's whole attention in order to extract the real and inmost thought of the *guru* are absolutely necessary.

Constant vigilance is necessary to keep oneself from the errors that may be committed in body, word, and mind.

To be empty of desire is necessary if one would remain independent.

He who will give no one the opportunity to grasp a rope hanging from his nose,[1] to lead him like an ox, must be freed from every kind of bond.

A natural tendency towards goodness and pity is necessary if one would always be disposed, materially or in thought, for the happiness of others.

§

Seek a master thoroughly enlightened in spiritual matters, learned, and overflowing with goodness.

Seek a quiet and pleasant place which appears to you suitable for study and reflection, and remain there.

Seek friends who share your beliefs and habits and in

[1]The rope represents desires, bonds.

whom you can put your trust.

Think of the evil consequences of gluttony and content yourself, in your retreat, with the amount of food that is indispensable for keeping you in good health.

Follow the régime and the mode of living that are calculated to keep you healthy and strong.

Practise such religious or mental exercises as develop your spiritual faculties.

Study impartially all teachings that are accessible to you, whatever be their tendencies.

Keep "the knower" within you ever fully active, whatever you may do and in whatsoever state you may find yourself.

§

Avoid a master who is ambitious, who aims at becoming famous or acquiring material possessions.

Avoid the friends, companions, relatives, or disciples whose company injures your peace of mind or your spiritual growth.

Avoid the houses and localities where people hate you or in which your mind is not at rest.

Avoid earning your living by deceiving or robbing another.

Avoid all actions calculated to injure or deteriorate your mind.

Avoid licentiousness and heedlessness which lower you in another's esteem.

Avoid conduct and actions which have no useful object in view.

Avoid concealing your shortcomings and publishing those of others.

Avoid actions inspired by avarice.

§

We must know that whatsoever befalls us – phenomena in general – is essentially impermanent. As the mind possesses no independent existence, no true "self", we must know that it is like space itself.

We must know that ideas (which constitute the mind) spring from a concatenation of causes, that speech and the body formed of the four elements, are impermanent.

We must know that the effects of past acts, from which proceed all moral sufferings, come about automatically. These sufferings may be one means of convincing the mind of the utility of the Doctrine (the Buddhist doctrine) which teaches the method of freeing oneself from suffering; consequently they must be recognised as spiritual teachers.

As material prosperity is frequently harmful to the religious life, we should look upon fame and prosperity as enemies against which we must be on our guard. As comfort and wealth, however, may also be the water and fertilising matter which favour spiritual development, we must not avoid them (when they offer themselves spontaneously).

As misfortunes and dangers sometimes drive the man who experiences them to turn to the Doctrine, they must be recognised as spiritual masters.

In reality, nothing that exists has an absolutely independent existence *per se*. All that exists in the universe: objects of knowledge that are formless or that possess form, ideas that enter the mind as consequences of impressions received through the senses, the circumstances of our life that come about as the result of previous actions – all these things are interdependent and inextricably blended together.

§

He who has become a religious man[1] should conduct himself as such and not simply assume a polish of spirituality whilst continuing to live like men of the world. He should leave his country and live in some place where he is unknown, in order to free himself from the tyranny of the home and from the ties produced by habitual intercourse and custom, in so far as men and things are concerned.

Having chosen a wise Lama as his master, he should reject pride and love of self, listening to his master's teachings and following his advice.

The religious man should not chatter to all and sundry about the teachings he has imbibed or the psychic exercises into which he has been initiated, but he should put them into practice in his daily life.

When he has glimpsed the inner light, he should not give way to idleness but rather make use of this initial gleam and never more remove from it the eyes of his mind.

When he has once tasted the bliss of contemplative meditation, he should seek calm and solitude for its practice and not sink back into the material activities and preoccupations of the world.

The religious man should be absolute master of his body, his speech, and his thoughts. Aiming after Deliverance, he ought never to seek his own interests (the interests of his "self" which he knows to be illusory)[2] but always to work for the

---

[1]The words *religion* and *religious* used in this translation possess for Lamaists a very different meaning from that which they have in the West. They do not refer to worship paid to a God in order to merit his favour, but rather to a method taught by sages of liberating oneself from illusion and of attaining spiritual enlightenment by one's own efforts.

[2]It is explained to disciples more advanced than those to whom these precepts are addressed, that he who aims after final liberation should not seek even his spiritual interest, or work for it. These rules are based on mystic theories which regard Deliverance as the transition to a state where all preoccupa-

interests of others. Not even for a single moment should he permit his body, his speech, or his thoughts to be applied to vulgar usage.

§

Beginners along the mystic path listen perseveringly to discourse concerning the Doctrine.

Faith in it having come to you, continue to make it the object of your meditations.

Persevere in solitude until you have won the power of contemplation.

If your thoughts wander and become difficult to concentrate, persevere in your efforts to master them.

If torpor overcomes you, persevere in stimulating and strengthening your mind.

Persevere in meditation until you have attained immovable serenity.

When you have succeeded in this, persevere in your efforts to prolong this state of mental serenity and to succeed in producing it at will, so that it may become habitual with you.

If misfortunes assail you, persevere in the threefold patience of body, speech, and thought.

If desires or ties spring up within you and are on the point of mastering you, crush them as soon as they manifest themselves.

If your feelings of benevolence and pity languish, restore them by the steadfast practice of good and charitable deeds.

§

tions, noble or ignoble, spiritual or material, based on the conceptions produced by our ignorance, cease to exist.

Reflect on the difficulty of being born a human being, and may this incline you to practise the Doctrine whenever you have the opportunity.

Think of death, of our uncertainty as regards the duration and the circumstances of our life, and may this incline you to live in accordance with the Doctrine.

May the thought of the inflexibility of the concatenation of causes and effects incline you to avoid actions that produce evil results.

Think of the vanity and insignificance of life in the round of successive existences, and may this thought incline you to work to liberate yourselves therefrom.

Think of the miseries of all kinds to which mortal beings are subject and may this incline you to endeavour to reach mental enlightenment (which delivers therefrom).

Think of the evil tendencies, the injustice and disloyalty latent in most beings. Think of the difficulty one has in uprooting these inclinations and destroying the erroneous impressions from which they arise. May these thoughts incline you to meditate so that you may attain to Reality.

§

The union of a weak faith with a highly developed intellect inclines one to fall into error, to become a mere coiner of phrases.

A strong faith combined with a feeble intellect inclines one to fall into error and to become a sectarian confined in the narrow pathway of dogmatism.

Great ardour without right teaching inclines one to fall into error and to adopt extreme and erroneous views.

The practice of meditation divorced from knowledge inclines one to fall into a torpor or state of unconsciousness.

Not to practise what one has learnt and recognised as the best instruction, exposes a man to become vain, imagining that he possesses intuitive science and looking upon all learning with disdain.

Not to feel considerable pity (for all who suffer) exposes one to fall into sheer intellectualism and selfishly to seek after personal salvation.

Not to keep one's mind on the intellectual pathway exposes one to follow the vulgar tracks of the world.

Not to stifle ambition exposes a man to allow himself to be guided by worldly motives.

He who takes pleasure in receiving the visits of those who admire and believe in him exposes himself to mean and petty pride.

§

Desire may be mistaken for faith.

A selfish attachment may be mistaken for love or compassion.

An arrest in brain activity or a state of unconsciousness may be mistaken for the ecstasy of the sphere of infinite mind.[1]

Phenomena supplied by the senses may be mistaken for the revelation of Knowledge.

Men giving way to their passions may be mistaken for *naljorpas* (mystics) who have liberated themselves from all conventional laws.

Actions with a selfish end in view may be mistaken for manifestations of altruism.

Disloyal practices may be mistaken for prudent methods.

Charlatans may be mistaken for sages.

---

[1] One of the Buddhist contemplations technically designated as "formless".

§

To tear oneself from all attachment to objects and to forsake home, devoting oneself to the homeless life of an ascetic, is not to commit an error.

To revere one's spiritual master is not to commit an error.

To study the Doctrine thoroughly, to listen to instruction, to reflect and meditate thereon, is not to commit an error.

To nourish lofty and noble aspirations, along with modest conduct, is not to commit an error.

To entertain liberal views, to be firm in one's resolutions and engagements is not to commit an error.

To combine an alert penetrating mind with a minimum of pride, is not to commit an error.

To combine erudition in philosophical doctrines, persevering energy in mastering them, intensity of spiritual experience and absence of vanity, is not to commit an error.

To combine abnegation and disinterested devotion with wise methods of doing good to others, is not to commit an error.

§

If, after being born a human being, one gives no thought to spiritual things, one is like a man who returns empty-handed from a land rich in precious stones. This is a grievous failure.

If, after entering the religious Order, one turns back to the life of the world and the pursuit of material interests, one resembles a moth burning its wings in the flame of a lamp. This is a grievous failure.

He who remains ignorant of the company of a wise man is like one who dies of thirst on the bank of a stream. This is a grievous failure.

To know the moral precepts and not to use them to counteract the effects of passions is to resemble a sick man carrying a medicine chest which he never opens. This is a grievous failure.

To talk religion without putting into practice what are songs is to initiate the prattling of a parrot. This is grevious failure.

To give in alms and charity property earned by theft, pilfering, robbery, and cheating, is like lightning flashing over the surface of water: a grievous failure.

To offer to the gods meat obtained by killing animate objects is the same as to offer a mother the flesh of her own child.

To simulate austerity and piety, to do meritorious works in order to attract the esteem of men and to win celebrity, is to barter a precious jewel for a mouthful of food.

To be skilled in the practice of spiritual exercises and yet to experience no inclination for them is to resemble a rich man who has lost the key of the room that contains his treasure.

To attempt to explain to others the meaning of spiritual truths or of treatises concerning the Doctrine which one does not perfectly well understand oneself, is to resemble a blind man leading the blind.

He who regards as of prime importance the sensations or the results whatsoever produced by physical practices, and loses sight of the realm of the mind, is like a man who takes a piece of gilt copper for pure gold.

§

Even though a religious man[1] may live in the strictest seclu-

[1]In what follows, this term does not necessarily mean an ordained member of the monastic Order, but whosoever has turned aside from the worldly life with the intention of advancing along the "Path of Deliverance" (*thar lam*).

sion, it is an error for him to have his mind filled with thoughts of the world and of the success it is possible to obtain therein.

When a religious man is the acknowledged head of a group of monks or laymen, it is an error for him to seek his own interests.

To be greedy or to have the slightest desire is an error for a religious man.

To make a distinction between that which pleases and that which displeases, not to reject all feelings of attraction and aversion, is an error for a religious man.

If, after having left ordinary mortality behind him, a religious man is still eager to acquire merits[1] he commits an error.

It is an error for a religious man not to persevere in meditation, once he catches a glimpse of Reality.

To abandon the search after truth is an error for the religious man who has taken a vow to discover it.

It is an error for a religious man if he does not reform anything blameworthy in his conduct.

To make a show of occult powers for healing sickness or to practise exorcism is an error for a religious man.[2]

To praise oneself cunningly and at the same time to disparage others is an error for a religious man.

To barter sacred truth for livelihood and wealth, is an error for a religious man.[3]

To preach lofty doctrines to others and to act in contra-

---

[1] This refers to the merits, and the rewards attached thereto, which the average man expects as the prize of his good deeds.

[2] This is a strictly Buddhist principle found in the oldest Buddhist Scriptures and set forth by the Buddha himself. It is but little observed by Lamaists.

[3] It is said that a master of mystical doctrines should refuse to teach them to one who is incapable of understanding them or unworthy to hear them, even though the latter should offer in exchange all the treasures in the world, and that, on the other hand, he should impart them freely to the disciple capable of making good use of them.

diction to what they teach, is an error for a religious man.

Not to be capable of living in solitude, to lack the firmness necessary to remain unperverted by ease, and to lack courage to endure poverty and want is an error for a religious man.

§

An alert and penetrating intellect capable of grasping the practical use to be made of the truths one has discovered, is indispensable.

A genuine aversion for the continual sequence of deaths and rebirths is absolutely necessary as the starting-point of the spiritual life.[1]

A master capable of being a sure guide on the path leading to Liberation is indispensable to the one who enters this path.

Deep understanding, indomitable courage, and steadfast perseverance are indispensable.

Keen penetration, capable of grasping the nature of "the Knower",[2] is indispensable.

The power to concentrate the mind upon any object at any place or time is indispensable.

The art of utilising any action to further one's spiritual progress is indispensable.

§

[1]Because the spiritual life, the Buddhists say, has for its object Deliverance from this round of successive existences.

[2]In Tibetan: *rnampar chespa*, one of the five principles (the combination of which, according to Buddhism, forms the personality), the principle of consciousness.

To have but little pride or envy denotes a pure nature.

To have but few desires, to be readily satisfied with objects of little worth, and the absence of pretence and hypocrisy, are the marks of a superior mind.

To regulate one's conduct in accordance with the law of cause and effect denotes intelligence.

To regard all beings impartially denotes a superior mind.

To be pitiful to – and free from anger against – those who indulge in evil actions, denotes a superior mind.

To leave victory to others and take defeat upon oneself, denotes a superior mind.

To differ from men of the world[1] in one's most insignificant thoughts, denotes a superior mind.

To behave hypocritically is like eating poisoned food; it is preparing oneself for suffering.

A feeble-minded man at the head of a monastery is like an old woman tending herds of cattle; he is preparing difficulties for himself.

Not to work for another's happiness and to make another serve one's own happiness is to resemble a blind man wandering in the desert and causing trouble for himself.

He who is incapable of successfully managing his own affairs and yet undertakes more weighty matters, is like a feeble

[1]This expression must always be interpreted in its religious sense; the one that it has in the Gospel when Jesus says: "I pray not for the world", or when he says of his disciples 'They are not of the world, even as I am not of the world' (John xvii, 9, 16). Here, the world is the domain of the search for material interests and of the ignorance of spiritual truths, as contrasted with the domain of philosophy and of effort in the conquest of Truth. Or else, as the Hindu Tantrikas brutally express it, the world is the domain of the *pashus* (animals). More politely the Tibetans generally call these "people of the world", "children", and sometimes, though less often, "fools". The distinction between the "sons of the world" and those who are "out of the world" is a very ancient one in Buddhism.

man who attempts to carry a heavy burden; he is preparing trouble for himself.[1]

The man who idles about the town and neglects meditation is like a chamois going down into the valley instead of remaining on the mountains where he is safe.

To work for the possession of earthly goods instead of developing one's mind is to resemble an eagle which has lost the use of its wings.

§

A man can congratulate himself when he is capable of breaking his links with the ordinary forms of religion in order to seek a master who is wise and noble.

A man can congratulate himself when he is capable of abandoning the accumulation of wealth.

A man can congratulate himself when he is capable of giving up social life and living alone in a place apart.

A man can congratulate himself when he is free from the desire for luxury and from ambition.

A man can congratulate himself when he is determined never to make use of others in the attainment of selfish ends and when he makes his behaviour conform to this determination.

A man can congratulate himself when he has weaned himself from form (from the objects of sense) and is bent upon penetrating to the nature of the mind.

§

[1]This refers to those who are not ready to understand the Doctrine or are incapable of living a spiritual life, and who begin preaching and gathering disciples about them.

Faith in the law of cause and effect is the best of considerations for a man of inferior[1] capacity for spiritual insight.

To recognise in all things, both within and outside of oneself, the working of universal energy and conscious mind, is the best of considerations for a man of medium capacity for spiritual insight.

To discern the fundamental unity of the Knower, the object of knowledge and the action of knowing[2] is the best of considerations for a man of the highest capacity for spiritual insight.

Perfect concentration upon a single object is the best form of meditation for a man of inferior intellectual capacity.

Continual reflection on universal energy and the conscious mind is the best form of meditation for a man of medium intellectual capacity.

To remain in a tranquil state of mind, all reasoning processes absent, knowing that "the one who meditates", the object of meditation and the act of meditating form an inseparable unity, is the best form of meditation for a man of the highest intellectual capacity.

To rule one's conduct by the law of cause and effect is the best form of morality and the best of all religious practices for a man of mediocre intellectual capacity.

Complete detachment, regarding all things as images seen in a dream, as unreal forms of a mirage, and treating them as such, is the best form of religious practice for a man of medium intellectual capacity.

---

[1]The context indicates that the terms "inferior" and "mediocre" must be understood in a relative sense. Here they do not signify an almost complete lack of intelligence, but only intelligence less keen than that possessed by those who apply to themselves the above maxims.

[2]In Tibetan: *Shespa-po*, *Shes cha* (written *Shes bya*), and *Shespa*. This is one of the fundamental theories of the Lamaist philosophy.

To abstain from all desires and actions is the highest form of religious practice for a man of the highest intellectual capacity.

The gradual diminution of egoism and ignorance is one of the best signs of spiritual progress in persons of all three grades of intellect.

§

If a man follows a hypocritical charlatan instead of a sage who sincerely practises the Doctrine, he makes a fatal mistake.

If a man makes far-reaching plans in the expectation of a long life, instead of carrying out his duties every day as though this day were the last that he has to live, he makes a fatal mistake.

If a man undertakes to preach religious doctrines before a large number of listeners, instead of meditating in solitude on the meaning of these doctrines, he makes a fatal mistake.

If a man gives way to a life of debauchery instead of practising purity and chastity, he make a fatal mistake.

If a man spends his life between vulgar fears and hopes instead of becoming aware of Reality, he makes a fatal mistake.

If a man attempts to reform another instead of reforming himself, he makes a fatal mistake.

If a man attempts to obtain a high social position instead of working at the development of the Knowledge latent within himself, he makes a fatal mistake.

If a man spends his life in idleness instead of seeking enlightenment, he makes a fatal mistake.

§

The first of necessary things is to feel a strong aversion from the continual succession of deaths and rebirths to which one is subject, and to desire to escape from the prison of repeated existences as ardently as an imprisoned deer wishes to escape from its cage.

The second necessary thing is stern and courageous perseverance which nothing can dishearten.

The third is contentment, joy in effort.

It is supremely necessary to understand that time is measured out to us like the last few moments of a man who has received a mortal wound.

Then it is necessary to reflect on this point.

Lastly it is necessary to understand that there is nothing to be done.

In the first place it is necessary to feel for the Doctrine as imperious a desire as that of a man hungering after good food.

Secondly one must understand the nature of one's mind.

Finally, one must recognise the error of duality, the fundamental identity of things.

§

Having recognised the empty nature of the mind[1] it is no longer necessary to listen to – or meditate upon – religious discourses.

Having recognised the pure nature of "intellect", it is no longer necessary to seek absolution for one's sins.

No absolution is necessary for him who enters the path of calm and peace.

He whose mind has attained a state of unalloyed purity[2]

---

[1]Here we are dealing with the doctrine which denies the existence of the "self". The mind is "empty" of "self". It is compound and impermanent.

[2]Purity is taken in the sense of perfect limpidity which permits of the vision of Reality, a vision which preoccupations, reasoning processes, desires, etc., blur by forming an opaque screen.

needs not to meditate upon the "Path" or upon the ways of entering it.

He who has thrown aside all passions no longer needs to continue opposing them.

He who knows that all phenomena are illusory no longer needs to reject or to seek anything whatsoever.

A FRIENDLY EPISTLE OF NÂGÂRJUNA

In the second collection of the Lamaic canonical books named the Tengyur (*bstan hgyur*) "commentaries", is the famous epistle attributed to the great Hindu philosopher Nâgârjuna whose philosophical doctrine exercises great authority among the Lamaists. A few passages from this epistle will now be given.

Whether Nâgârjuna was really the author of this letter, or it was written by one of his disciples or by someone who used his name, need not now be discussed. We would simply note that the short course of morals of which it consists, although Mahâyânic and recommended by the Tibetan *gurus*, is quite conformable with the teachings of primitive Buddhism.

§

Keep thy body, thy speech, and thy mind along the path of the ten virtuous actions.[1] Abstain from intoxicating drinks and

---

[1]These ten virtuous actions are: (1) not to kill any living being; (2) not to steal; (3) not to have unlawful sexual relations; (4) not to lie; (5) not to slander; (6) not to speak harsh or evil words; (7) not to indulge in frivolous or aimless conversation; (8) not to be greedy or give way to covetousness; (9) not to be cruel in deed or intent; not to entertain evil designs; (10) not to entertain false opinions.

take delight in living by honest means.[1]

Knowing that riches are perishable and fleeting, give liberally to the poor, to thy friends in need, and to ascetics. Nothing is so good as charity, it is the best of friends for our companionship and sustenance in lives to come.

Esteem chastity highly, do not pollute or degrade thyself by coarse actions. Chastity of mind is the foundation of all virtues, as the earth is the support of all living beings and motionless things alike.

May boundless charity, chastity, vigilance, and serenity be thy portion. And may wisdom, adding to them its might, by their aid traverse the ocean of the world, bringing thee nearer to the Buddhic state.

Revere thy father and mother, thy good friends and thy masters. Such acts of respect win fair renown and subsequently a happy rebirth.

To cause evil, to wound, to rob, to lie, impure actions – drunkenness, gluttony which impels one to eat at unseasonable times, soft luxuriousness which inclines one to recline on easy couches, singing, dancing, and adornment – all these must be given up.[2]

Since by these observances one follows in the footsteps of the Arhats and prepares for oneself a birth amongst the gods,

[1]As the letter was addressed to a ruling prince, he would not need to earn his livelihood. All the same, he could see that imposing burdensome taxes in order to provide for luxuries was forbidden by the Buddhist law, as also was engaging in war in defence of his throne. Buddhists are forbidden to engage in five sorts of commerce: the sale of arms, the sale of living beings (even of animals), the sale of flesh meat (as a butcher), the sale of fermented drink, and the sale of poisons, intoxicating drugs, etc.

[2]To eat outside the appointed hours, i.e. after the hour of noon, to recline on high and soft beds, singing, dancing, adornment and perfumery are forbidden to members of the religious Order of the Buddhists, though not to faithful laymen. In what follows, the writer of the letter urges his correspondents to preach the excellence of these observances to laymen also.

teach them to the laity, both men and women.

Regard as thy enemies: avarice, disloyalty, envy, arrogance, hatred, anger, pride of rank, of beauty, of wealth, of youth, or of knowledge. Regard power as an enemy.

Those who have led a licentious or criminal life and, recognising their wrongdoings, have transformed their conduct, assume a beauty like to that of the moon emerging from the clouds.

No austerity is equivalent to patience, therefore never allow thyself to be carried away by anger.

Whilst we are thinking: "These men have insulted, blamed or overcome me, those have ruined me," anger and fury are born within us. Therefore throw aside these resentments and sleep in peace.

Know that the mind upon which images are drawn may be like water, earth, or a store.[1] When evil passions rend thee, it is better that the mind should be like water.[2] For the man who follows truth, it is better that it should be a safe store.

There are three kinds of words: those that are pleasant, those that are true, and those that are false. The first are like honey, the second are like flowers, and the third are like impurities. Avoid the third.

Some men go from light to light, others from darkness to darkness. Some pass from light to darkness and others from darkness to light. Be thou amongst the former.

Learn that men are like the fruit of the mango-tree. Some appear ripened (wise) who are anything but ripe. Others, although ripened, do not appear at all ripe. Others who are by

[1]In Tibetan *mdzod*, pronounced *dzöd*; every place where things are kept in reserve: a treasury, various objects, corn stored against famine, etc. The whole of the things kept in reserve is also called *mdzod*.

[2]In order that these feelings may not persist, that they may disappear immediately, like a drawing traced upon water.

no means ripe appear unripened and others again, being ripened, appear as ripened. Learn to discriminate between them.

§

Amongst the various philosophical systems in Tibet one of the most highly reputed is the one called *Chag gya chenpo*.[1] It consists of the knowledge of the superior doctrine of the essential unity of all things, combined with the practice of works that draw their inspiration from this doctrine. The esoteric meaning of the word *chag* (phyag) is the Void or the absence of all qualities, of all conditions of existence which can be represented by words or imagined in thought, since words and thoughts can express only limited things and what is meant by Void is the Absolute. The word *gya* (rgya) esoterically means the liberation the disciple attains by a knowledge of this doctrine. The meaning of *chenpo*[2] is here the union of this superior knowledge of the fundamental unity of all things and liberation from the works of the world. Such are the explanations given by the masters who teach the *Chag gya chenpo*, and they are confirmed by the works of ancient authors who professed this doctrine in past centuries.

To relate the historical origins of this philosophical system is outside my subject; I will confine myself to stating that it is of Hindu origin, is connected with the (*dbuma*)[3] philosophy preached by the master Nâgârjuna, and that it was introduced into Tibet by the Grand Lama of the monastery of Sakya: Sakya Penchen and by other religious masters.

[1]Written *phyag rgya chenpo*. Literally: the "great gesture" or the "great sign".
[2]Literally *chenpo* means "great".
[3]Its original Sanskrit name is *mâdhyamika*, "of the middle" – the doctrine which rejects extreme views.

The counsels on the method of meditating summarised below are given to their disciples by the Lamas who profess the doctrine of the *Chag gya chenpo*, after having conferred on them an appropriate *angkur*.

I borrow from them my own notes taken down from the words of several of these Lamas; I have also consulted a work which they hold in great esteem, entitled *Chag chen gyi zindi* (*phyag tchen gyi zin bris*). This is a guide, a kind of reference book for the use of those who seek salvation along the path of the *Chag gya Chenpo*.

§

After seating oneself in a quiet and solitary spot, one will first remain motionless and tranquil, without making the slightest mental effort; without proposing to meditate and preparing to carry out a spiritual exercise as one thinks: "I have come here to meditate. . . . I must carry out the task of meditation." This tranquillity of body, speech, and mind which no effort keeps in tension and which has no goal in view, is called: "allowing the mind to remain in its natural state".

It is said:[1]

"Think not of the past.
 Think not of the future."[2]

"Think not: I am meditating.

 Imagine not the Void as being Nothingness."

[1] The author of the *Chag chen gyi zindi* quotes other works and also precepts which oral tradition attributes to famous masters whom, however, he often omits to mention.
[2] This precept is attributed to Tilopa.

Whatever be the impressions felt by the five senses, one must not, for the moment, seek to analyse them; on the contrary, the mind must be left in perfect repose.

It is said:

"By refraining from forming notions or ideas referring to objects perceived,
    By leaving the mind in repose, like a little child's,[1]
    By zealously following the advice of one's spiritual guide,
    One will certainly obtain understanding of the Void and be set free from the works of the world – these two things coinciding."[2]

Tilopa said:

"Do not imagine, do not reason, do not analyse;
    Do not meditate, do not reflect,
    Keep thy mind in its natural state."[3]

The master Marmidze said:

"Absence of distractions (perfect attention) is the path followed by all the Buddhas."

This is what is called tranquillity of mind, the immobility of the mind remaining in its natural state (or remaining in its real abode).

Nâgârjuna said:

---

[1] The comparison would not seem to be a very happy one. The mind of a child is generally very active.
[2] The understanding of the Void is liberation itself.
[3] These six precepts were given by Tilopa to his disciple Narota.

"Remember that attention has been declared the only path the Buddhas have trod. Observe constantly thy body (the actions performed by the body, the activity of the five senses, their causes and results), in order to know it.

Neglect in this observation makes all spiritual exercises of none effect.

It is this continual attention that is called: freedom from absent-mindedness."

It is said in the Abhidharma:

"Memory (enjoined on the disciple) consists in never forgetting the beings or things with which one has been in contact."

§

After having experienced mental tranquillity, it is fitting to concentrate the mind upon a single point.

One of the methods leading thereto may be practised with the aid of some tangible object or without making use of any material object.

In the former case, the object may be a small ball or a stick.[1] In the latter case, one may concentrate the mind on the bodily form, the word or the mind of the Buddha.

The way to use material objects is as follows:

Place before one a small ball or a stick on which to concentrate one's thoughts.

Do not allow the "knower"[2] to stray from this object or

---

[1]The *sgom ching* mentioned in *With Mystics and Magicians in Tibet*.
[2]This principle is sometimes called in Tibetan: *Shespa-po* and sometimes *yid kyi rnampar shespa*.

wander around, or enter into him[1] but regard it fixedly, without allowing the thoughts to turn aside from it.

Then meditate upon one's spiritual master, i.e. form an image of him and keep the mind fixed upon him.

If one feels tired, overcome by torpor or sleep, one should persist and steady the gaze, meditating in a place from which a vast stretch of country may be seen.

If, on the other hand, the mind wanders, one must shut oneself up in one's hermitage and, with downcast eyes, keep one's mind tranquil by ceasing from all effort, as previously explained.

When one takes for one's object the bodily form, the speech or the mind of the Buddha, they are imaged as follows:

For the body, one uses a small statue or a painted picture, representing the Buddha.

For the speech, one uses a syllable.

For the mind, one uses a point.

It is possible to dispense with statue or picture, and visualise the form of the Buddha. Then he will be imagined as clad in a religious costume, surrounded with light and always present before one.

Concentration upon speech comes about by visualising the image of a circle of the size of a nail on which is inscribed the syllable *hrî*[2] in strokes as thin as a hair.

Concentration upon the mind comes about by imaging in front of oneself a point which is as large as a pea and sends out rays of light.[3]

[1]This refers to the psychic experiences in which one identifies oneself with an object. See *With Mystics and Magicians in Tibet*, Chapter VIII.

[2]*Hrî* is a mystic term that has numerous esoteric explanations. It signifies the universal uncreated essence of things.

[3]All these rules, the reasons upon which they are based, etc., should be accompanied by the explanatory commentaries of a Lama well acquainted with the system.

§

Included in the exercises taught to the novices (the preliminary or elementary teaching) is that of dismissing a thought at the very moment it is born; also that of allowing it to continue without giving it form (without halting to make of it a mental image).

When one meditates, one perceives that many ideas, one after the other, come into being with extreme rapidity. Therefore, as soon as a thought begins to sprout it must be cut off at the root, then meditation must be continued.

By continuing meditation and gradually prolonging the duration of the periods when the formation of ideas does not take place, one finally notices (what had not hitherto been noticed) that by the involuntary formation of ideas, they tread on the steps of one another, as it were, and form an endless succession.

This discovery of the involuntary formation of ideas equals the discovery of enemies.

The condition, then, which one reaches is like that of a man, standing on the bank of a river, watching the water flow past. The tranquil and observing mind thus watches the passage of the uninterrupted flow – like the water of a stream – of the ideas that follow close upon one another.

If the mind reaches this state, though only for a moment, it understands the birth and the cessation of mental formations.

It then appears, because they have been observed – and formerly one was unconscious of the fact – that the mental formations become more numerous, but this is not so.

That which is outside of the arising of mental formations and instantly puts an end to this arising, is Reality.

In the second place comes the exercise, which consists in

leaving unformulated the ideas that arise.

Whatever be the idea that offers itself, no attention must be given to it; it must be left to itself without allowing oneself to be influenced by it, without reasoning about it and also without seeking to divert it. The mind thus resembles a shepherd tending a flock and continues meditating.

By persevering in this way, mental formations no longer appear and the mind reaches the state of tranquillity, of one-pointed concentration.

The master Gampopa (a name of Dagpo Lha Dje) said:

"When the mind is left relaxed, it becomes quiet,
When nothing disturbs the water, it becomes limpid."

The ascetic Milarespa, the Lord of the contemplative anchorites, said:

"By leaving the mind in its natural state, without causing it to assume form,[1] the first drawings of Knowledge are seen to appear.

By keeping the mind relaxed, flowing like the peaceful water of a river, Reality is reflected therein."

The sage Saraha summed up this dual process of meditation in the following lines:

"When the mind is kept bound, it endeavours to wander

---

[1]This must be interpreted as referring to the ideas, the ways of thinking and seeing which various influences force upon the mind, the result being that it assumes an artificial conformation. It is like a stream of water which is diverted from its course, its bed being widened out or narrowed by dikes or dams, or like a tree that is pruned, or has its branches forced down, etc.; thus being robbed of its natural form. (Explanations given by Lamas.)

in the ten directions.

When it is left free, it remains motionless.

I understood that it was a baffling animal, like the camel."

§

The higher teaching includes meditation upon *that* which in the mind remains motionless and upon *that* which is in motion (the spectator and the actor).

(1) The mind must be observed in its state of quiet repose. (2) We must examine the nature of this motionless "thing". (3) We must examine *how* that which is called mind remains in repose, and *how* it moves by quitting its tranquillity.

We must examine: (1) whether motion comes about in the mind apart from the state of tranquillity; (2) whether it moves even when at rest; (3) whether its motion is or is not something different from immobility (the state of repose).

We must examine what is the kind of reality of this motion, and then what conditions cause this motion to cease.

We reach the conclusion that *that* which moves is not different from *that* which remains motionless.

Having reached this point, we must ask ourselves if the mind which observes *that* which moves and *that* which remains motionless is different from them, if it is the "self" of that which moves and of that which is motionless.

We then ascertain that the observer and the thing observed are inseparable. And as it is impossible to classify these two realities (the observer and the thing observed) as being either a duality or a unity, they are called "the goal beyond the mind" and "the goal beyond all theories".

It is said:

"However noble they may be, the goals created by the

mind are perishable.

And *that* which is beyond the mind cannot be called a goal."

In the Sûtra entitled: *The Questions of Kashyapa*, we read:

"By rubbing two sticks against each other, fire is produced.

And by the fire born of them, both sticks are consumed.

Likewise, by the intelligence born of them,

The couple formed by 'the motionless' and by 'the moving', and the observer who considers their duality, are alike consumed."

This meditation is called: "The hermit's discerning meditation." It should not be mistaken for "the savant's discerning meditation" because the latter examines things from without.

The doctors of the *Chag gya chenpo* also teach the means of utilising for one's spiritual progress the obstacles calculated to check it; in addition, they teach many ways of analysing the mind:

Is it a thing composed of matter?

If it is material, of what kind of matter is it made?

If it is an objective thing, what is its form, its colour?

If it is a "knower", is it an idea that manifests temporarily?

What then is this *immaterial* thing which manifests in different forms?

What is that which produces it?

If the mind were a genuine entity, it would be possible to consider it as a kind of substance.

After still further considerations, one arrives at the conclusion that the mind is neither material nor immaterial, and that it does not come under the category of those things of which it can be said that *they are* or *they are not*.

The questions still continue and we come to the inquiry as to the compound or non-compound character of the mind.

Is the mind a simple thing?

Is it a compound thing?

If it is simple, how does it manifest in different ways?

If it is compound, how can it be brought to that state of "void" in which there is no longer anything but unity?

Continuing our investigations, we come to recognise that the mind is free from both the extremes of unity and plurality.

"In the quiet state of the man who has reached this understanding, the result of meditation is attained; to him all things appear as illusory as the forms produced by a mirage."

It is said:

"Before me, behind me, in the ten directions,
  Wherever I look, I see 'That itself.'[1]
  Today, O master, the illusion has been scattered;
  Henceforth I shall ask nothing of anyone."

I might multiply quotations and extend this chapter to an indefinite length. The original Tibetan works are not lacking. Those that I have brought to France would already keep several translators occupied throughout their lives. But what is this poor collection compared with those contained in the

---

[1] *Te jine ñid* (written *de bchin ñid*) "that itself", i.e. the Reality.

great libraries of Tibet, where the numbers of volumes, piled up century after century, may be counted in hundreds of thousands?

My aim in supplementing the present volume by the translation of a few Tibetan texts has simply been to lead my readers to the threshold of those esoteric schools of Tibet regarding which so many fabulous reports have been spread, and to introduce them to some of the teachings which the Lamas give to their disciples.

Needless to say, the theories expounded in the above-mentioned fragments of text are not the only ones accepted in these schools. One may judge of this from my explanations when describing the "initiations". Nevertheless, the unity of views, amongst enlightened Lamaists, is far greater than one might be led to suppose from the various doctrines preached in Tibet by missionaries of the various Mahâyânist or Tantric sects. The centuries have brought about a certain fusion between all these doctrines, and Tibetan mentality has strongly impressed upon them its own particular stamp.

In a word, the Buddhism of the Lamaists, released from its popular forms, is dominated by a spirit as alien to the classic Hînayâna as to the devout and sentimental Mahâyâna which some have set up as the only genuine Mahâyâna of Asanga and his successors.

Just as among the patriarchs of the Ts'an sect we find the fundamental principles of Buddhism, envisaged and developed by Chinese brains and impregnated by them with the Chinese spirit, so we also find among the philosophers and mystics of Tibet these same fundamental principles envisaged and interpreted from the point of view of a people mentally very different from the Indians.

Which of his disciples have most correctly expressed the thought of the Buddha? – That is a problem not at all easy to solve, for we lack the necessary elements upon which to base our judgement. The documents that refer to the teaching of the Great Sage, Siddhartha Gautama, the Buddha, are far subsequent to the period at which he lived, and we are justified in regarding them as strongly tinged with the opinions and tendencies which then prevailed among the Buddhist monks.

Those who attribute this to the Buddha ancestors among the Yellow races, or among the non-Aryan races more or less related to them, will probably think that his distant cousins of Central Asia or the Far East are more naturally fitted than others to apprehend the full meaning of his doctrine. Such a question, if it is ever to be solved, at all events cannot be solved in a few lines.

Should circumstances permit, I shall perhaps examine it some day; still, whatever be the conclusions one may reach on the matter, they will never possess a character of absolute certainty.

We may therefore believe that, while taking care not to neglect interesting historical and philosophical investigations, we may well follow the advice set forth in the Lamaic "initiations", and reach, by means analogous to those which he himself used, the Reality contemplated by the Buddha, and, instead of asking another for the secret of this master's thought, to make it our own by becoming Buddha ourselves.

12

THE TIBETAN
INTELLIGENTSIA

In many of the works which have been written on Tibet we are given descriptions, often inaccurate, of the various classes of the population. There is, however, one of these which is hardly ever mentioned, I mean that of the *literati*, the Tibetan intelligentsia as we might call them. They form a little world of their own, very self-contained, almost inaccessible to the outsider and hidden in a country which now, more than ever, is forbidden to the visitor.

Despite the ideas that have been spread in the West concerning the so-called "mysteries" that the Tibetan monasteries shelter, it is not among the monastery monks that may be found the great experts in magical rites or the erudite theoreticians of occult doctrines. Most of these live solitary lives, independent, and either remain quite alone or continue to reside near their families for such men do not, of necessity, belong to the regular clergy and may well be married.[1]

[1] Padmasambhava who first preached Buddhism in Tibet (eighth century) was a layman. Marpa (the spiritual master of the celebrated ascetic and poet Milarespa) together with Dagpo Lha Dje, the founders of the sect of the Khagyudpas, were married, as are many of the *naldjorpas* (*rnal byor pa*) – that is "those who have attained unto serenity" – and all the *nagspa* (*snagspa*) or "possessors of secret magic formulae." In the case of these men "initiation" takes the place of clerical ordination.

If, as often happens, their parents place them, as children, in a monastery where they get their education, later on, they forsake the great monastic institutions so as to enjoy solitude and silence.[1]

Few of the Tibetan intellectuals are ascetics. The Buddha inculcated moderation and detachment, but condemned asceticism whose futility he himself had recognised after a long and painful experience.

The dwelling of a Tibetan scholar is generally comfortable but without any display of luxury. The owner's artistic tastes are often shown in a fine collection of *thangkas*, those scrolls or rolls which we often call by the Japanese name of *kakemono*. On an altar against one of the walls of the main room will be a statue of the Buddha as well as that of some well-known mystic, the *Yidam*[2] of the master of the house, also, possibly, the representation of a former Grand Lama, the spiritual ancestor of the philosophical school to which the owner belongs. This altar will be provided with the customary

---

[1] Although it is possible to live there in a very retired and independent way as the author of this book has done. In *Mystiques et Magiciens du Tibet* as well as in *Mon Voyage à Lhassa* and others of my books there will be found descriptions of the Tibetan monasteries. They are often miniature cities inhabited by several thousand monks – there are, for instance, about ten thousand at Depung. Each one of the monks lives in his own apartment, according to his income, either in a great palatial mansion, a house that is unpretentious though comfortable, a modest lodging if the monk is not well off, or again a single, humble cell. Neither vows of poverty nor of obedience are taken. Except for an obligation to attend certain services at which there are ritual recitations of the Scriptures, the members of the monastery are free to do what they like until sunset by which time all must have returned to the compound and have retired to their apartments. After curfew all noise is forbidden.

[2] The *Yidam* corresponds more or less to the *ishta devata* of the Hindus, that is to say the divinity with which the devotee maintains special relations of love and adoration, but there is this difference, the *Yidam* is not an object of adoration but a subject of meditation.

ritual objects, for generally speaking, and through indifference, the Tibetan intellectual although freed from all superstition, avoids, making himself conspicuous by advertising an incredulity which he has no desire to communicate to others. The finer spirits, the *rabs*, will, so he thinks, come to share this incredulity without being persuaded thereto.

The scholar will maintain a resident monk whose business it is to perform the ritual of the "cult" that is to say to place, at dawn, bowls filled with pure water before the images on the altar, to empty these bowls at night and to replace them with lamps fed with butter.

The master of the house absorbed in reading or in meditation will pay not the slightest attention to the monk's acts.

Those of the *literati* who will allow a few disciples to approach them, summon them often at evening and will explain a text while unfolding for these disciples the teaching which the scholar himself received from his master: or he will converse with them and discuss matters of literature or philosophy. Such meetings often last far into the night. A bowl of tea is drunk[1] before the disciples withdraw, and then the master, once more alone, will read or meditate often until day breaks.

There are a few *literati* to be found among that clerical aristocracy which is peculiar to Lamaism and is called *tulkus* or in Mongolian *hutuku*.[2]

These *tulkus* having been recognised – generally speaking in their infancy – as reincarnations of some eminent

---

[1]Those masters who belong to the Tantric sects serve grain spirit instead of tea and the former is often drunk out of a human skull cut in the form of a cup and not seldom lined with silver. The author of this book owns several of these which have been so used in Tibet.

[2]The Chinese use this latter title in their official acts and it was given to my adopted son the Lama Yongden.

personage of the past, become, as of right, the heirs of his property, his titles and his prerogatives and take up their quarters in his dwelling which may be a sumptuous palace or a simple though comfortable house, as the case may be.[1]

A *tulku* who gives himself up to literary studies, to philosophical meditations or who is drawn towards investigations into magic, will have in his house a room apart where he is able to be alone, the excuse being that he is engaged in the respected practice of *tsam*.[2]

There is nothing to prevent a scholarly member of the clergy from travelling. For centuries past the example has been given by those who have resided in India, China or Nepal. If these travellers are *tulkus*, then they keep their official domicile at the headquarters of the founder of the line of reincarnations to which they belong.

Among the *tulkus* are to be found a few erudite men with very open minds and very subtle and acute understanding, but

[1] Whom foreigners often call, most improperly, "Living Buddhas". There is no reincarnation of the Buddha but only a series of supposed reincarnations of Lamas distinguished for their learning or their sanctity.

[2] *Tsam* (*mtsams*) means "barrier" or "frontier". *Tsam* is practised more or less strictly in the following manners. (1) By retiring into a cave or a hut erected in a desert place and living there alone. Food is brought from time to time to the hermit and laid at his door without his being seen or heard or any word being addressed to him. (2) The *tsampa* may speak to his visitor without seeing him, or may pass him a written note to inform him of what may be needed. (3) The *tsampa* may shut himself up in two rooms of his house. His meals and anything else he may need are placed in one room while the *tsampa* remains in the other room without being seen. (4) The *tsampa* may see those who serve him and may speak to them but he does not receive any other visitor. (5) The *tsampa* who lives in a very solitary spot may leave his cave or his hut to walk about in the neighbourhood, but he must hold no communication with anyone and he must avoid being seen. All the members of the higher clergy who live religious lives, or who affect to do so, make a retreat from time to time as a *tsampa*. A Lama who occupies a rank of some importance is expected, at least once during the course of his life, to pass three years, three months and three days in more or less rigorous *tsam*.

most of them spend their time in their sumptuous dwellings in a state of dull beatitude. Often they are, like their lay fellow-countrymen, avid of gain and engage in commerce through their stewards or through professional merchants whom they finance. They take their cue from the highest authority, for the Dalai Lamas have always derived important and large revenues from the capital they entrust to traders.

We may, no doubt, include also among the Tibetan intelligentsia certain anchorites who live in caverns or in huts generally situated at a great altitude, sometimes right up to the snow-line.[1]

Such men are called *gomchén* (*sgomtchén*) which means "great thinker" or "great meditator". Among them may be found a few philosophers who have been induced by peculiar circumstances to retire into complete solitude. These men may be remarkable both by their erudition and by the deep significance of their views. But such *gomchén* are few in number and most of these anchorites are given over to practices aimed at acquiring magical powers or which are simply dictated by superstition.

Anchorites, furthermore, are becoming fewer and fewer in Tibet; the conditions favourable for them are to be found with increasing difficulty;

> "Facing the mountain lake,
>   Back against the mountain rock,"

and a view that admits of the sun's rising and setting being seen from the door. Such is the ancient rule regarding the site of a hermitage. Moreover, the view that is spread before the

---

[1] The line of perpetual snow lies well above 10,000 feet in the Himâlaya and in Tibet.

hermit must contain no human habitation.

Such conditions are rapidly disappearing in Tibet. Irrigation, prospecting, the exploitation of sub-soil riches and the construction of motor roads, have all led to settlements being made in regions until lately quite deserted.

Which, we may inquire, among the different philosophical schools of Buddhism, is that held in most honour by the Tibetan intellectuals? Most of these men are idealists, adopt the views of Nâgârjuna (second century AD) and profess complete agreement with the closing words of the Prajñâpâramitâ, the great work of which Nâgârjuna is the reputed author:

"Like images seen in a dream, thus we must regard all things."

This concept is widely held even outside the circle of the intellectuals properly speaking. We meet with this idea, indeed, among all those Tibetans whose religion is on a higher plane than that of the popular rites and ceremonies. A story from the autobiography of the poet and ascetic Milarespa[1] illustrates this.

One day Milarespa on returning to the cave that served him as a lodging and after he had busied himself with some things he had to do outside, saw therein a number of demons who were engaged in wantonly destroying his little store of food and books. He admonished them to no effect; then he endeavoured to reason with them. "I have made you no offerings," he said. "Do not be angry with me, I do not always

---

[1]That is "Mila who is dressed in cotton" (*ras*, pronounced *rés* means "cotton"). Such a robe, a thin cotton garment worn during the coldest weather, is the distinctive sign of adepts in the practice of *tumo* (*gtumo*) an art that is designed to provoke the development of internal warmth.

forget to do this, I had not any intention of offending you."
But neither threats nor arguments produced any effect upon
the demons which went on with their work of destruction.
Then Milarespa, who had meanwhile realised the situation
more clearly, apostrophised himself: "O Mila, was it really
worth-while to have spent so many years in meditation and still
believe in the existence of demons? Do you not know that they
are a product of your own creation and exist only in your
mind?" Then, addressing the demons, he said "Do then what
ever you want to do." At once the demon shapes vanished.

The doctrine set forth in the Prajñâpâramitâ is considered by Tibetan intellectuals as the ultimate expression of the
highest wisdom. Although this is not the place to discuss, from
the grammatical point of view, the exactness of the Tibetan
translation, we may mention that Prajñâpâramitâ is rendered
in Tibetan as *Shesrab kyi pharol tu chinpa* (*Shés rab kyi pharol
tu phyin pa*) that is to say "Going beyond Knowledge". A
whole programme of philosophical conceptions and of practical discipline is based upon this "going beyond". While the
Sanskrit term *pâramitâ*, taken in its usually accepted sense of
"excellent" or "superior" is applied as such to a whole series
of virtues, according to the Tibetan text the aim is to "pass
beyond" them. The number of these virtues was originally six,
later on four others were added – they are: Charity (Alms),
Morality, Patience, Skill, Concentration of the Spirit,
Meditation and Knowledge. While the four additional virtues
are Method, Wishes (Vows),[1] Mental Power, Wisdom.

Although the excellence of these ten virtues is unani-

---

[1]Wishes, or vows, in Tibetan *meulam* (*smonlam*) and in Sanskrit *pranidhana*,
occupy in Buddhism a place analogous to that of prayers in theistic religions.
Buddhists do not pray, they wish and in general, they believe that if the
mental power of him who expresses the wish is sufficiently intense, such a
wish acquires efficiency and produces the realisation of the result desired.

mously recognised by the Tibetans and the practice of them highly recommended, the masters who base their teaching upon "going beyond knowledge" apply this to each of the ten virtues. It is not only the question of practising them but of "going beyond" them, of passing beyond all religious and social codes.

One passes "beyond" virtues and codes, not by disobeying their injunctions but by recognising their relative nature. One passes "beyond" when it has been realised that such virtues and codes are but the products of concepts formed in the spirit of men deceived by the erroneous conclusions of their senses; when it has been understood that the "Six Excellent Virtues" as well as all codes in no way partake of Absolute Truth but are the work of men and drawn up in special circumstances, things which other and different circumstances may deprive of all value.

Very few, say the Tibetan spiritual masters, have come to realise the relative character of all precepts, of all teaching and the relative and illusory nature of their own persons and of the world in which they move. Very few are those who have, also, understood the necessity of conforming their conduct to such a condition of things, false from the point of view of Absolute Truth, but true from that of Relative Truth, the only truth which is suitable for or accessible to them.

The Tibetans lay particular stress upon this distinction between the two sorts of truth,[1] on the one hand an Absolute Truth which, if it exists cannot be expressed or even conceived ("outside the sphere of thought" as the Tibetan texts have it) and Relative Truth based upon the knowledge gained by investigation, by experience, a truth that we are advised to cul-

---

[1] Absolute Truth: *don dompa* (in Sanskrit *paramârtha satya*). Relative Truth: *kundzob* (*kunrzob*), (in Sanskrit *samvrittisatya*).

tivate with assiduity so as to avoid the suffering arising from failure to recognise such truth.

Not all are able to attain this discernment and therefore the Tibetan intellectuals are much inclined to give an esoterical character to the doctrines they profess. The Buddha, however, is strongly denied having kept secret any part of his teaching. The canonical scriptures recount that, when he was nearing his end, and when his cousin Ânanda asked him if he had not some further instructions to give, the Buddha answered unambiguously:

"What then do the disciples think, ânanda. I am not like those masters who keep their hands clenched. I have preached all the Doctrines both esoteric and exoteric."[1]

Indeed, there cannot be really in Buddhism any secret doctrine. All the original doctrine of the Buddha as well as the diverse interpretations of it are exposed in the canonical scriptures and in the books which are read with them. Esoterism, say the most enlightened of the Tibetan spiritual masters, is created by the varying degrees of intelligence existing among those who listen.

These auditors are classed by the masters into three categories: the *thama*, that is to say common, obtuse-minded men; the *ding* (*hbring*), men of average understanding who by diligent effort may succeed in clarifying their mental vision; and

---

[1] We read however elsewhere (in the *Samyuttaka Nikâya*): "The Buddha finding himself with his disciples under a *sinsapa* tree, plucked several of its leaves in his right hand and said: 'What think you are the more numerous, the leaves I hold in my hand or those which are on the tree, above us?' 'Those which are on the tree are more numerous, Master' 'So it is with the things I have discovered and have not declared unto you. And why have I not so declared them? Because they do not lead to deliverance from suffering.'" I do not think that the Tibetan Masters make use of either of these two texts.

the *rab*, superior men who are at once able to comprehend.

This classification is supported by a text which relates that after he had attained spiritual Enlightenment, the Buddha hesitated to declare the facts which had appeared to him, since he felt that he would not be understood and that his teaching would revolt those who were "immersed in ignorance and slaves of their coarse desires". The text describes for us, farther on, the Buddha viewing the world as a lotus pool, "some lingering in the mud at the bottom of the pool, others coming almost to the surface of the water so that their flower is but little wetted, while still others raise their flowers in glorious fashion far above the water."

"Thus, thought the Buddha, there are men whose mental eye is covered with a thick layer of dust, some whose mental eye is veiled by but a thin sprinkling of dust, while there are again others whose mental eye is free from all dust."[1]

And, for the benefit of those capable of understanding it, the Buddha decided to teach his doctrine. It is this same attitude which is adopted by the masters belonging to the Tibetan intelligentsia regarding the doctrine of "passing beyond".

It would be imprudent, they hold, to reveal, indiscriminately to one and all, that, really, there is neither good nor evil, that both are but conventions of a relative character. The vulgar would conclude from this that they were at liberty to indulge, without any restraint, their base instincts. The constraint exercised by conventional moral principles, although these are fundamentally false, is necessary for the maintenance of peace and for the well-being of the mass of ordinary men.[2]

The conclusion to be drawn from this attitude is that the

---

[1] I have heard a comparable opinion expressed, in picturesque fashion, by a Westerner who knew nothing at all about Buddhism: "Religion is necessary," he said, "for women, children and servants."
[2] *Mahâvagga.*

Buddhist doctrine is not for the use of the majority of men, but that it is suited only for an intellectual aristocracy.

For the mass of Tibetan Buddhists there exists, undoubtedly, knowledge which is impossible of attainment. Such knowledge is held to be communicated only from master to disciple during a course of teaching which consists of progressive "initiations" such as those described in this book. The fundamental principles of Buddhism form always the basis of this teaching. We may briefly recall those principles.

First of all the essentially transitory nature of all groupings of elements. The absence, to any degree whatsoever, of a permanent homogeneous principle, completely distinct from the various component parts of the grouping, and which takes the form of a unit.

In primitive Buddhism these principles were expressed by two Pali words *anicca* and *anatta* that is to say "impermanence" and "absence of *ego*". The Tibetans have enlarged this formula so as to underline still farther its absolute and definite character. They repeat: 'There is no *ego* in the individual, there is no *ego* in anything.'

Then, among the fundamental principles of Buddhism comes the recognition of suffering, discovered in all its forms, either potentially or developed in all things and described briefly as: (a) to be deprived of what one loves, that is to say of what causes agreeable mental or physical sensations, and (b) to be in contact with what is displeasing, that is to say, with what produces disagreeable or painful sensations.

Once the existence of suffering is recognised, there follows a revolt against it. We should note here that the Buddhist attitude differs from that of most religions and philosophies. These, indeed, recommend either a resigned acceptance of suffering considered as being unavoidable and inevitable, or a submission of a religious character in which suffering is held to be an expiation, "the wages of sin" or some inexplicable manifestation, which must not be questioned, of the will of a god.

The Buddhist rejects both of these views and recommends a refusal to suffer and the will to rid oneself of it.

After the realisation of the existence of suffering and after the will to rid oneself of it, there comes the search for the cause of suffering. This cause is described in the form of an enumeration of twelve articles, the "Interdependent Origins":

SANSKRIT	TIBETAN	ENGLISH
avidyâ	marigpa	Ignorance
samskâra	dudjé (*hdubged*)	Concepts, ideas, literally "assemblage"
vijñâna	namparshespa (*ramparshespa*)	Consciousness, knowledge
nâma rupa	ming tang zug (*ming tang gzugs*)	Name and form (explained as the sphere of things mental and that of material objects)
sadâyatana	kyé ched tug (*skyé thed drug*)	The six senses and their objects, the domain of perception, the spirit being counted as a sixth sense
sparsa	régpa	Touch, contact
vedanâ	tsorwa	Sensation, perception
trishna	sédpa (*srédpa*)	Desire, thirst
upâdâna	lénpa	Attachment, prehension
bhâva	sipa (*sridpa*)	Existence, as "becoming"[1]
jâti	kyéwa (*skyéwa*)	Birth
jarâ-marana	ga-shi (*rga-shi*)	Old age, death

[1]Existence in the absolute sense of being (Sanskrit, *sat*. Tibetan, *yeu* (*yod*).

The qualificatory term "interdependence" added to the word "origins" is of importance. We should not, of course, think that each of the above articles follows that which precedes it by a sort of filiation, or that the one is *produced* by the other. The conditions set out above, one after the other, exist in dependence on each other. "That being so, this happens," say the texts. Ignorance is not exactly *produced*, it exists simultaneously with all the other "origins".

A discipline formulated in eight articles is presented as the "Noble Way" that leads to the suppression of suffering:

On the superior plane of teaching and understanding which is supposed to be that of the Initiations, the interpretation given to the doctrines set out above, differs very greatly from the popular conception of them. Thus, the chain of interdependent origins, commonly considered as applying to living

SANSKRIT	TIBETAN	ENGLISH
samyagdristi	yand dag païl tawa	Right views
samyaksamkalpa	yand dag païl togpa	Correct
	(*yang dag pahi rtogpa*)	reasoning
samyagvâk	yang dag païl ngag	Correct words.
samyakkarmânta	yang dag païl les kyi ta	Correct aims
	(*yang dag pahi les kyi mthah*)	
samyagâjiva	yang dag païl tsowa	Correct con-
	(*yang dag pahi htsowa*)	duct
samyag-vinyâma	yang dag païl tsolwa	Correct
	(*yang dag pahi rtolwa*)	means
samyaksmriti	yang dag païl tenpa	Perfect mem-
	(*yang dag pahi drenpa*)	ory
samyaksamâdhi	yang dag païl ting gné dzin	Perfect medi-
	(*yang dag pahi ting gné hdzin*)	tation, concentration of the spirit

beings and showing their progress from life to life through reincarnations, takes on a universal character. Birth is not only that of an individual human, animal, divine or demon – such anthropomorphism is set on one side. Birth means a phenomenon of manifestation of any sort, within the sphere of existence, a transitory manifestation that declines (old age) and disappears (death) while the forces from which it issued and those which it has aroused by its activity, appear again in analogous or different forms (re-birth).

We may notice here, that the most ancient Buddhist sects, those of the Theravadins established already a distinction between those who follow the "paths of the world", the *puthujjana* and those who follow the "paths outside the world", the *lokuttara*.

All the teachings making up the body of the doctrine are considered as comprising two meanings, one, adapted to the "world" that is to say to the degree of comprehension and to the needs of the mass of those who listen, and another meaning adapted to the "beyond the world" and comprehensible to those whose mental faculties are more highly developed. As things exist at present in Tibet there is no question of a double teaching but only of the degree of understanding of those who receive the one teaching.

Some men, of their own accord, make for the "direct path", the perilous path that demands an exceptionally sure foot. They climb the mountain by following a straight line. This is the path of rapid spiritual illumination, the sudden flash of understanding that the Japanese of the Zen sects call *satori*. Other men, again, set off on the long road of moral observances and practise virtue according to the guidance of their spirits vitiated by ignorance. This is the path that leads by a circuitous way up the mountain. Is the summit ever reached by this path? The reply to this question is ambiguous in Tibet as it was already in India. As it is said in the Bhagavadgîtâ: "Those who venerate the gods, move towards the god. Those who seek for knowledge move towards knowledge."

But even when all the teachings have been accepted and meditated upon, even when the disciple has passed "beyond" and he looks, in fact, upon the world as "images seen in a dream", there still remains for him to pass "beyond the beyond". *Gaté, gaté, paramgaté parasamgaté* says the mantram of the Prajñâpâramitâ. That "beyond the beyond" is it not the realisation of the fact that this "beyond" with the load of ideas that we attach to it, is still only a concept elaborated by our spirit, a "confection"[1] as it is called in the Buddhist scriptures, and that, after all, we continue to wander among the fancies of our imagination?

What then? . . . The last thought is never formulated in words. *Mré sam djö med*[2] "I think of speaking, but there are no words" (to express it).

This silence is that of the supreme beatitude described as being at once "without thoughts and without absence of thoughts", like the void and that which is voided of the void . . . *Nirvâna*.

Thus is Buddhism understood among the intelligentsia of Tibet.

---

[1] Sanskrit *samskara*: Tibetan *dudjé*.
[2] Written *smra bsam rdjod med*.

APPENDIX

A NOTE ON THE PRESENT[1] SITUATION OF THE DALAI AND THE PENCHEN LAMAS

The remarks in Chapter 5 dealing with the Dalai Lamas indicate, I think, well enough the real position that these pontiffs occupy in Lamaism. However, we may inquire whether the political events in China and their influence in Tibet have modified the former state of things. The answer is that these events have merely brought back the situation to what it was before. The Dalai Lamas, indeed, as temporal rulers of Tibet, were a creation of the Chinese. Before there were any Dalai Lamas, the Grand Lamas of the Sakya monastery exercised such a temporal sovereignty, when about 1240, the Emperor Kublai Khan constituted the most erudite Sakya Pandit as king of the four Tibetan provinces of U, Tsang, Amdo and Khams. The Sakyapas, although supplanted by the disciples of Tsong Khapa, still exist in Tibet and enjoy the reputation of being "specialists" in the occult sciences.

Neither Tsong Khapa nor his immediate successors[1] at the head of the *Gelugspas* "yellow caps" enjoyed temporal power, neither did they bear the title of Dalai Lama which was

---

[1] *i.e. 1958, the date of the previous edition.*
[2] *Kas dup djé* (*mkhas grub rjê*) and *Gédun dub* (*dge dun grub*).

239

conferred in 1577 by Altan Khan, a Mongol prince (*Dalai* means "Ocean" in Mongolian), on the *third* successor of Tsong Khapa who was called Sönam Gyatso.[1]

However, the older, non-reformed sects, the "red caps", were alarmed at the progress of the "yellow caps" whose adepts, becoming ever more numerous, endeavoured to destroy the influence of the Red Caps. In order to ward off the danger to the old Red Cap clergy – whose protector he had constituted himself – the Prince of Tsang occupied Lhasa where the fifth successor to Tsong Khapa, Ngawang Lobzang (Ngag Dbang Blobzang) had his abode. Ngawang Lobzang applied for assistance to the chieftain of one of the Mongol tribes living near the Koko Nor in the present Chinese province of Chinghai. This chieftain and his allies invaded Tibet, defeated the enemies of Ngawang Lobzang – the "red caps" and the Böns.[2] The Grand Lamas of Sakya were deprived of their sovereignty and Gushi Khan the Mongol chieftain, conferred upon Ngawang the temporal power over the central provinces of U and Tsang.

We may note that, this time, Khams and Amdo were left out of the fiefs assigned to the Grand Lama of Lhasa and the fact is that the provinces of Khams and Amdo have never been really subject to the government in Lhasa and have retained until this day a semi-independence under local rulers more or less dependent upon the Chinese authorities.

The Chinese never renounced their suzerainty over Tibet and indeed claimed it specifically even when, on several

---

[1] Sönam Gyatso, signifies "Ocean of merit or virtue". The Mongol term *dalai* (ocean) corresponded therefore to the title *gyatso* which the Lama already bore.

[2] Bön is the name given to the followers of the ancient religion of Tibet before the introduction of Buddhism. The doctrines of the Böns may be regarded as Shamanism with elements that suggest Taoism.

occasions, the Tibetans, for a short time, managed to expel Chinese troops from the central provinces of Tibet. Now, under the title of an "autonomous region within the Chinese Republic", Tibet has reassumed its old position as a vassal of China, but, also, as in the past, Tibet has as its nominal sovereign, a Dalai Lama with a Chinese resident whose function is to indicate what shall be the behaviour of the ruler and his ministers.

The young man (he is still only twenty-one years of age) whose singular destiny it is to reign at Lhasa, is of humble origin and a native of the frontier province of Amdo whose inhabitants, much cross-bred with Chinese and Mongols, do not much resemble the Tibetans of the central provinces. Many of the inhabitants of Amdo spoke Chinese as children, before they learned Tibetan, and, in fact, a large number of the monks at the celebrated Amdo monastery of Kum Bum, never learn Tibetan at all.

The career of the new Dalai Lama began in circumstances very different from those known by his predecessors who spent their youth confined in the Potala and saw no one but their masters charged with the task of teaching the rulers to recite by heart the text of many books of ritual and doctrinal treatises whose meaning was never explained. The present Dalai Lama, however, has not only made a prolonged stay in Peking, but the celebration of the two-thousand five hundredth anniversary of the Buddha's birth furnished the occasion for the sovereign's suzerains to permit him to visit India. As a companion the Dalai Lama was given the other Grand Lama of Tibet, the Penchen Lama to whom the Chinese have restored his official Mongolian title of Penchen erdeni. He is a few years younger than the Dalai Lama and, like him, is a native of the Amdo province. A Chinese mentor was provided whose task was to watch over the young men's activities and to tell them what speeches they had to make, what attitude they had to adopt in the various circumstances occurring during the programme of their visit. There were receptions, banquets, visits to interesting places, artistic and sporting occasions. In fact the Dalai Lama and the Penchen Lama were plunged into a veritable whirlpool of festivities. We may imagine how flattering it must have been for them to be received with deference by the President of the Indian Republic, the Prime Minister, the Governors of the various States and a number of distinguished persons celebrated for reasons that are quite unknown to the inhabitants of Amdo. The young men appeared to be enchanted with their stay. Their faces were beaming when they got out of their plane and, amid plaudits of welcome, they raised their hands in acknowledgement as do Western sovereigns.

The Dalai Lamas of old, secluded and rigid as befitted their semi-divine character, are indeed far to seek. A new political régime has brought about an entirely new state of things in the lofty country of snows and mysteries.

We may inquire whether this new world will abolish the 'Initiations' that have been described in this book. The answer must be, certainly not. For a long time to come, the Tibetan spiritual masters will remain attached to the traditional rites that are used in these "Initiations". Even if an intellectual revolution should occur, as great in its own sphere as the other revolution that is changing the physical aspect of the Tibetan wilderness, such an intellectual revolution would produce only a modification in the forms and ceremonies beneath which is hidden the secret of the initiations.

This secret which transforms the outsider, bound by illusions, into one who sees clearly, into an "initiate", is described by the Tibetans in two words *lags thong* that is "to see more". The fruit of the "initiations" is the gift of being able to see more than the mass of men, to discover in all things what remains unperceived by most of us, to find out who *really* is the person we think ourselves to be and what really is the world in which we move.

To see more in order to know more is the final aim of "Lamaist Initiation".

§

Since this Appendix was written in 1958 much has changed in Tibet. The Dalai Lama has fled to India with his retinue, where he lives in exile. Tibet is garrisoned by the troops of Red China who actively patrol the frontier with India. Accurate knowledge of the situation in the interior is hard to come by.

1966.